MARLBORO McLAREN

MARLBORO McLAREN

TAG and Honda-powered Grand Prix Cars, 1983-90

Anthony Pritchard

Photographs by Nigel Snowdon and Diana Burnett

ASTON PUBLICATIONS
Sole distributors for the USA
Motorbooks International
Publishers & Wholesalers Inc.

Published in 1990 by
Aston Publications Limited
Bourne End House, Harvest Hill
Bourne End, Bucks, SL8 5JJ

ISBN 0 946627 59 2

Designed by Chris Hand

Printed in Hong Kong

Sole distributors to the UK book trade
Springfield Books Limited
Norman Road, Denby Dale
Huddersfield
West Yorkshire, HD8 8TH

Sole distributors for the United States
Motorbooks International
729 Prospect Avenue, Osceola
Wisconsin 54020
United States

CONTENTS

Introduction

Between 1984 and 1989, six seasons of racing, a McLaren driver won the World Championship five times (Niki Lauda once, Alain Prost three times and Ayrton Senna once) and the McLaren team won the Constructors' Cup four times. Only the strength of Williams in 1986 and 1987, when that team was still using Honda engines and enjoyed the talents of both Nelson Piquet and Nigel Mansell, prevented a 'grand slam' by McLaren International.

Ron Dennis has built and maintained the most successful racing team ever known in the history of Grand Prix racing and his own reputation as a team leader is also second to none. McLaren's success was built on a wide range of factors: Dennis's own vast experience as a mechanic and operator of his own team before his take-over of McLaren International, his fierce determination and ambition, his ability to organise and to choose the right personnel; the design and development abilities of first John Barnard and, latterly, Steve Nicholls; the significant financial involvement of Marlboro, and, since 1988 the technical input of Honda.

During the years 1984-87 McLaren astounded (and demoralised the opposition) by their brilliance. In 1988-89, however, that brilliance has been clouded by controversy, the out and out hostility between Alain Prost and Ayrton Senna and the growing conflict between McLaren International and FISA (the Federation Internationale du Sport Automobile, the governing body of motor sport). It is a conflict that I believe is only in its early stages as these words are written, a conflict between the achievers of power and the holders of power. McLaren International's appeal against Senna's disqualification in the 1989 Japanese Grand Prix *may* quietly disappear or it may be, apparently, amicably settled, but I believe that this is a conflict that will continue in 1990 to the ultimate detriment of FISA and the benefit of the sport.

This book is not intended as a detailed treatise of the development of McLaren International (that can only happen when Ron Dennis opens the portals – and the archives – with frankness to a motor racing researcher in whom he has complete confidence and trust and when the battles on and off the track have become history rather than news). It is, however, I hope, a full photographic record backed up by accurate statements of fact.

As I have so often in the past, I have to express my gratitude for the use of Nigel Snowdon's photographs. Those up until the end of the 1987 season are the property of Aston Publications, and those from 1988 to 1990 have been supplied by Nigel himself.

Anthony Pritchard
Ruislip
December 1989

1: McLaren: The First 17 Years

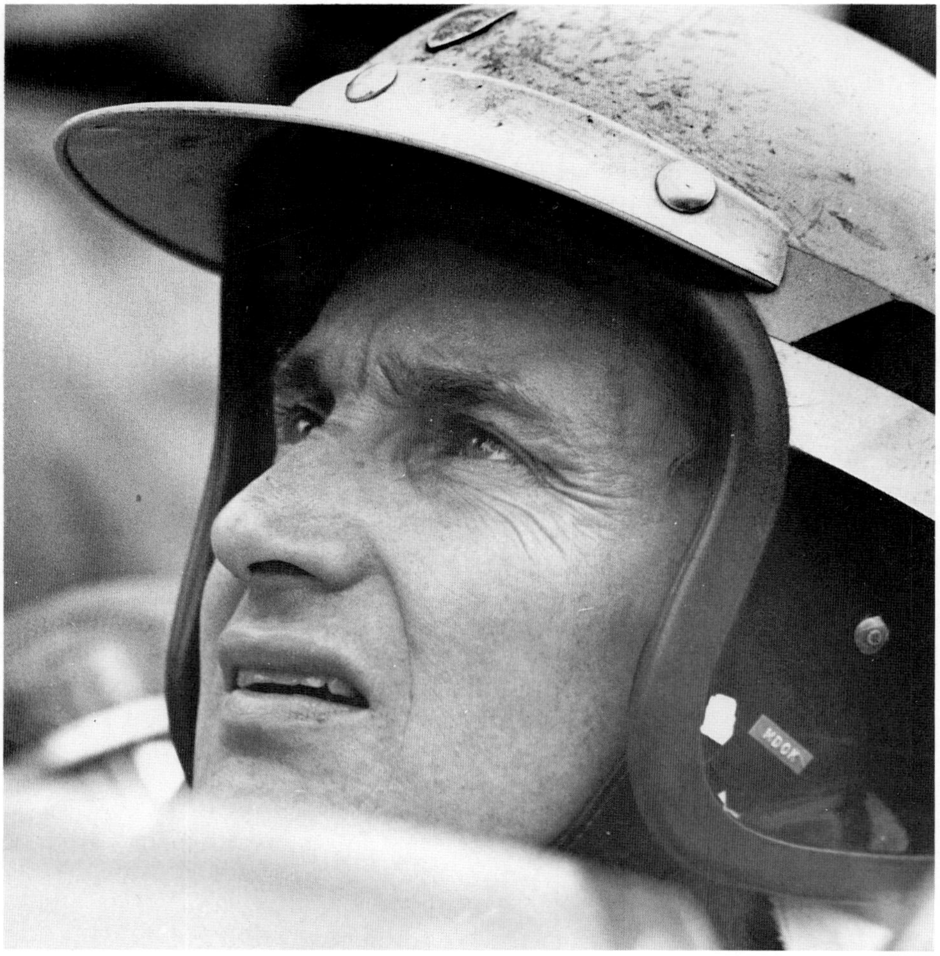

Bruce McLaren was a member of the works Cooper team between 1959 and 1965, but he acquired the ex-Penske Cooper Zerex in 1964 (which he entered as a Cooper-Climax) and later that year there appeared the first McLaren Group 7 car, the M1A. McLaren became dominant in Can-Am racing and this domination continued after McLaren's tragic death in testing at Goodwood in June 1970. Eventually McLaren withdrew at the end of 1972 in the face of turbocharged opposition.

In 1966 McLaren entered Formula 1 with the M2B designed by Robin Herd and featuring Mallite construction and a linered-down Ford V8 Indianapolis engine. Team colours were white with a broad green stripe. The design was unsuccessful and in a few races McLaren used the Serenissima V8 sports car engine. Here, in the British race in which he finished sixth, McLaren with a Serenissima-powered car leads Ligier's Cooper-Maserati.

While a new Formula 1 car was under development in 1967, Bruce McLaren raced a version of his M4A Formula 2 car powered by the 280 bhp 2.1-litre BRM V8 engine and known as the M4B. In 1967 the cars were painted red with a white nose-band. McLaren is seen at Monaco where he finished fourth. He also drove an Eagle for Dan Gurney during the year and the new M5A with BRM V12 engine made its début in the 1967 Canadian Grand Prix.

For 1968 Denis Hulme, the reigning World Champion, left Brabham to drive for McLaren and with the exception of the South African Grand Prix, in which Hulme drove the M5A, two cars were entered in all the year's Championship races. This photograph of Hulme was taken in 1973. He retired from Formula 1 at the end of the following year.

The 1968 car was the M7A with Cosworth DFV engine and painted orange. This is Denis Hulme's car at the French Grand Prix at Rouen where he finished fifth. In the race the car was fitted with a long range fuel tank on the right side only.

During 1969 McLaren continued to race the M7A early in the season, but also introduced the M7C with Formula 5000 monocoque. There was only the one of these cars and it was always driven by McLaren himself. Here McLaren is seen in practice at Monaco with high wings front and rear. These were banned prior to the race in which Bruce McLaren finished fifth. For 1970 the M7C was sold to John Surtees.

An expensive and wasteful development was the 1969 M9A four-wheel drive car designed by Jo Marquart. Its only race was the British Grand Prix in which it was driven by Derek Bell.

The 1970 Formula 1 car was the M14A, based on a simplified version of the M7C monocoque. It was a bad year for the team, for, apart from the tragic death of Bruce McLaren, Hulme suffered bad burns on his hands at Indianapolis. The team withdrew from the Belgian Grand Prix and Hulme also missed the Dutch race. After appearing for the team in the Race of Champions, Peter Gethin was entered by the team for most of the year's races following McLaren's death and Dan Gurney also drove for McLaren in four races. McLaren failed to win a single race in 1970. Here is Dan Gurney in the Dutch Grand Prix in which he retired with engine trouble.

During 1970 McLaren also entered M7D and M14D cars with Alfa Romeo V8 engines driven by Andrea de Adamich and (in one race) by 'Nanni' Galli. This is Andrea de Adamich (M14D) in practice for the German Grand Prix for which he failed to qualify as a starter.

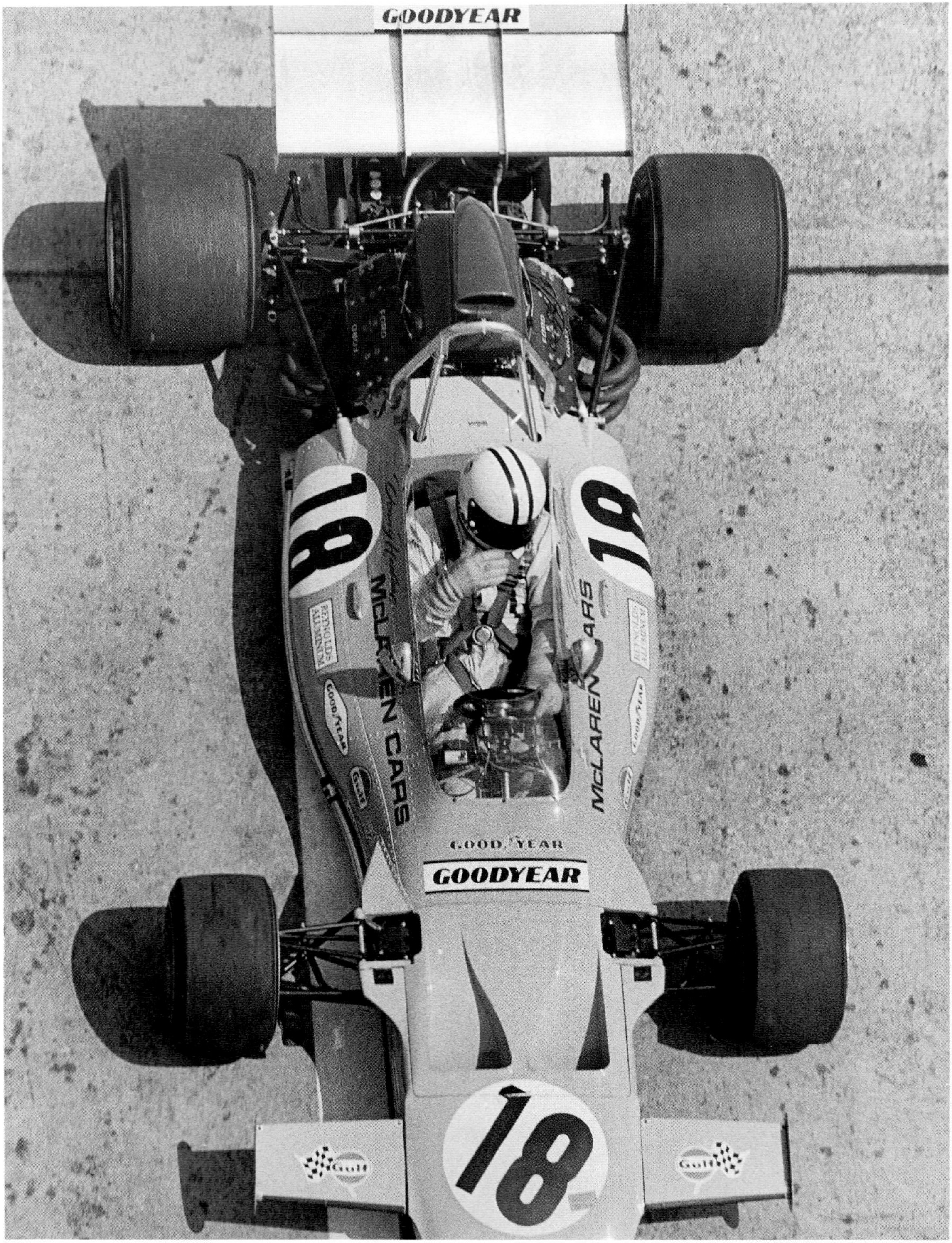
GOODYEAR
18
McLAREN CARS
18
McLAREN CARS
GOOD YEAR
GOODYEAR
18

Opposite: For 1971 former Brabham designer Ralph Bellamy drew up the M19A with longer wheelbase, Matra-style 'coke bottle' lines and rising rate suspension. Hulme led the South African Grand Prix until four laps before the finish a bolt fell out of the rear suspension, but again the team failed to win a single race that year. Here Denis Hulme is seen at the German Grand Prix at the Nürburgring where he retired.

McLaren continued to race the M19As in 1972, now with Yardley sponsorship, but also built two lighter M19C cars. Here Hulme is seen with M19C/1 in the French Grand Prix at Clermont-Ferrand where he took a poor seventh place. Peter Revson had joined the team alongside Hulme, but Brian Redman also drove for the team during the year. The team's best performance was a win by Hulme in South Africa.

For 1973 Gordon Coppuck designed the M23 to comply with the new deformable structure fuel tank protection regulations. Here Peter Revson, in his second season with McLaren, is seen with his right hand on the rear wing of his M23 at the British Grand Prix at Silverstone. The race was stopped after South African Jody Scheckter, at the wheel of a third M23, triggered off a multi-car accident on lap 2. Revson won the restarted race.

In 1974 there were in effect two McLaren teams, Texaco-Marlboro whose M23s were driven by Emerson Fittipaldi (the 1972 World Champion) and Hulme, while a single Yardley-sponsored M23 was driven by Mike Hailwood managed by Phil Kerr. Fittipaldi is seen on his way to second place in the British Grand Prix at Brands Hatch. Although Fittipaldi won only three of the year's races, he took the Drivers' World Championship and McLaren won the Constructors' Cup.

Although the Yardley team was much less successful, Hailwood did achieve some good places. He is seen on his way to his best result of the year, third place in the South African Grand Prix.

In 1975 McLaren raced the M23 for the third successive year and following Hulme's retirement Emerson Fittipaldi was partnered by Jochen Mass. A steady, reliable driver without the scintillating flair of a potential World Champion, Mass, seen here with rear wheels airborne, was awarded first place in the Spanish Grand Prix after the race was red-flagged with 29 laps completed following Stommelen's bad crash. Fittipaldi refused to start the race because he was unhappy with the safety arrangements.

At the end of 1975 Fittipaldi left McLaren to drive for his brother Wilson's Copersucar-sponsored team. His place was taken by James Hunt, seen here with the M23 and Teddy Mayer on his right. Jochen Mass stayed with the team, but faced with Hunt's competitive edge, lost his form.

James Hunt, seen here in the 1976 Spanish Grand Prix, in which he took pole position, was disqualified because the width of his car exceeded that permitted but then was reinstated. He won that year's World Championship.

In 1977 McLaren relied for most of the year on the old M23 now in its fifth season of racing. The new M26, designed by Gordon Coppuck with honeycomb construction chassis and hip radiators, lower and lighter than the M23, had a protracted development curve and achieved little in 1977. At the British Grand Prix, however, Hunt drove the M26 to pole position on the grid and first place.

McLaren also entered an M23 at Silverstone in 1977 for newcomer Gilles Villeneuve. Villeneuve was fastest in a pre-qualifying session for newcomers and private entrants, took ninth place on the grid and finished 11th after a pit stop.

In 1978 Hunt was joined in the McLaren team by Patrick Tambay and at certain races by Bruno Giacomelli who had first appeared for the team at Monza in 1977. It was a catastrophically unsuccessful year for the team. This is Giacomelli in the French Grand Prix at the Paul Ricard circuit where he retired his M26 because of engine problems.

The next stage in McLaren development was the ground effects 1979 M28 with Nomex honeycomb monocoque. It proved too big, too slow and, initially, lacked in rigidity. It was abandoned in mid-season in favour of the M29. Here at Monaco is John Watson who had joined Tambay in the team. He finished fourth with the M28, one of his best performances of the year.

The M29 was a close copy of the successful Williams FW07 with slim monocoque and a single central fuel cell. In the face of strong opposition McLaren failed to win a single race in 1979-80. By 1980 Tambay was thoroughly disillusioned and his place in the team that year was taken by Alain Prost. Prost is seen with the M29 in the 1980 Austrian Grand Prix in which he finished seventh.

The last model produced by Team McLaren Limited was the M30, an advanced ground effects car with much stiffer monocoque, inboard suspension and outboard brakes front and rear. It made its début in the 1980 Dutch Grand Prix and was written off in practice at the United States race at Watkins Glen that year. It was always raced by Alain Prost, seen here at Monza where he finished seventh.

Late in 1980 Team McLaren Ltd and Ron Dennis's Project Four Racing Ltd merged and the combined organization was known as McLaren International. Two years later Dennis bought out Mayer's shareholding and assumed control of McLaren International. The 1980 car was the MP4/1 designed by John Barnard with advanced carbon-fibre monocoque. The drivers in 1981 were John Watson and Andrea de Cesaris. Ron Dennis and John Watson are seen at the 1981 South African Grand Prix.

In 1981 the team's fortunes were much improved, although only one race was won. Here John Watson is on his way to a win in the British Grand Prix at Silverstone, McLaren's first win since the 1977 Japanese Grand Prix.

For 1982 Watson was joined in the team by Niki Lauda and the team raced the improved MP4/1B cars. During the year Watson and Lauda each won two races. This is Watson at Monaco where both McLaren entries retired.

2: 1983: The First Turborcharged Cars

The merger between Team McLaren and Ron Dennis's Project Four Team had first been suggested by Dennis in 1979 and rejected by McLaren. When he came back a year later with the same suggestion, Teddy Mayer of McLaren, under pressure from sponsors Marlboro, was forced to agree to the arrangement and so the new McLaren International company was formed in the early part of September 1980. Mayer, who had owned 85% of Team McLaren, remained the single largest shareholder in McLaren International with 45%. He was also Chairman, but both he and Dennis were joint Managing Directors, with both Tyler Alexander and designer John Barnard holding directorships. Barnard had at one time worked for McLaren, but had left to work on Jim Hall's Chaparral projects. He had then returned to England to work for Project Four because Dennis had been planning to extend the existing operation for Formula 3 and Formula 2 cars into Formula 1 and Barnard was to be the designer.

Barnard had already conceived what was to be the new McLaren MP4/1 ('Marlboro Project Four') and now at McLaren he created it for the 1981 season. The basis of the new MP4/1 was a very light, very stiff carbon-fibre monocoque which, because of production difficulties in Europe, was manufactured for McLaren International by Hercules Incorporated of Salt Lake City, Utah and around this monocoque the team built up their cars. Initially powered by the Cosworth DFV engine and with McLaren/Hewland gearbox, they were developed and raced from 1981 through to 1983, disabusing critics of the notion that the structural use of carbon-fibre gave poor impact resistance and the monocoques survived many a crash without problem.

By the end of 1982 Teddy Mayer – and Tyler Alexander – had both left McLaren and Ron Dennis was firmly at the helm. By this time negotiations were well advanced with Techniques d'Avant Garde, a company set up to invest Saudi oil revenues controlled by Akram Ojjeh, whereby Porsche were to be commissioned to build a turbocharged engine for the exclusive use of McLaren International. The TAG-Porsche 80-degree V6 of 1499cc was said to have a power output of about 700 bhp at 11,500 rpm in 1983 form and was the seventh turbocharged engine to appear in Formula 1, joining Ferrari, BMW, Hart, Renault, Alfa Romeo and Honda.

Throughout most of 1983 McLaren International's drivers John Watson and Niki Lauda relied on the familiar MP4/1C cars with the now obsolescent Cosworth engines and in a consistent year were probably the best of the Cosworth runners, despite problems with their Michelin tyres, and the successes during the year included, unexpectedly, first two places in the United States Grand Prix (West) at Long Beach, California.

In the meanwhile development work was progressing on the TAG engine, strictly in accordance

McLaren's only win in 1983 and the last with a Cosworth engine – which the team had been using since 1968 – was in the United States Grand Prix (West) at Long Beach. John Watson, seen here, took first place with the MP4/1C ahead of team-mate Lauda.

with Barnard's requirements. A new company, TAG Turbo Engines, had been formed to work contractually with Porsche and to sell the engines to McLaren International and the prototype engine was running as early as December 1982. Porsche installed the first engine in a 956 Group C coupé which was extensively tested at Weissach, contrary to the wishes of McLaren International who had wanted all the testing to be in their own Formula 1 chassis. Porsche believed that many lessons would be learned in this way; Barnard was convinced that running the engine in this chassis was something of a blind alley, because the 956 did not run under the same structural loads as would a Formula 1 car. He later concluded that this test period with the 956 delayed discovery of a serious throttle-lag problem. So far as the drivers, Watson and Lauda, were concerned, both

A delighted Watson after his Long Beach victory.

John Watson with the MP4/1E during testing at Brands Hatch in early September 1983.

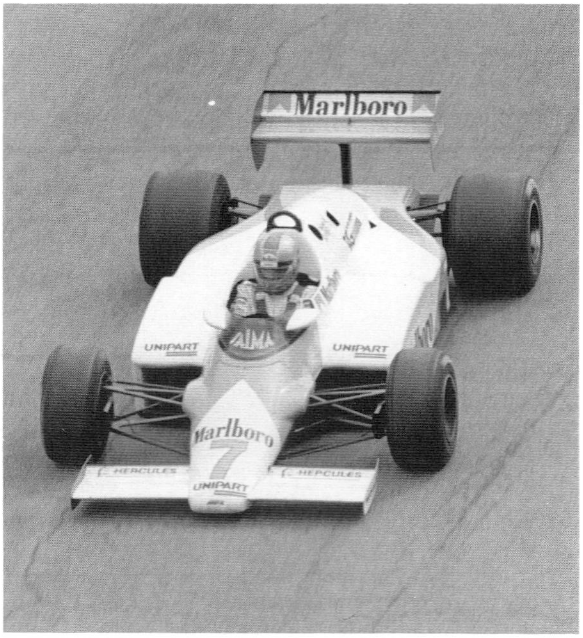

By the Italian Grand Prix in 1983 both McLaren drivers had the 'interim' turbocharged cars. This is Watson who retired because of valve gear failure.

tried the 956/TAG extensively and both were rather bemused by its lorry-like handling characteristics and impressed by its sheer power.

In the meanwhile, McLaren International had modified the original prototype carbon-fibre chassis, MP4/1-1, as a test hack for the turbo engine and it became the MP4/ID. Whilst Barnard wanted to continue development with the hack, the team had made assurances to their sponsors that the cars would be raced in 1983 and so with some reluctance he had to agree to the building of two new interim cars, MP4/1E-01 and MP4/1E-02, based on former MP4/1C Cosworth-powered monocoques.

Lauda drove the first of the new cars in the Dutch Grand Prix at Zandvoort on 28 August, qualifying 19th and retiring on lap 26, when holding 14th place, because of boiling brake fluid. By the Italian Grand Prix a fortnight later McLaren had a second car ready for Watson and now iron brake discs had been substituted for the team's usual carbon brakes. At Monza Lauda qualified 13th and Watson 15th, but both cars retired. Watson was in seventh place after 13 laps when the valve gear failed and Lauda was eliminated by electrical problems, when holding 20th and last place.

By the European Grand Prix at Brands Hatch, a number of changes had been made to the cars, including the adoption of a much larger new wing, and modified turbochargers, radiators and exhaust pipes. Watson retired because of failure of the rear wing and Lauda was eliminated by another failure of the valve gear.

The final race of the season was the South African Grand Prix at Kyalami where a third MP4/1E was brought along as a spare and this was based on the MP4/1C-07 Cosworth chassis. Throughout qualifying the engineers struggled, without any obvious success, to make the McLarens start and run properly and prospects in the race looked poor indeed. For Watson there was to be no race as such, because although he started and completed 18 laps, he was disqualified for a breach of race regulations. The reason was that he had switched to the spare car at the last moment, there were great problems in getting the engine to fire and instead of joining up at the back of the grid, he worked his way towards his grid position as the field completed its final parade lap. There was however, to be some encouragement for the team after a disappointing display so far in 1983, for Lauda's steady driving brought him through to second place, but he dropped out six laps from the finish because of electrical problems. He was classified 11th.

The potential of the TAG engine was only too obvious, but it was equally obvious that a great deal of development work was needed to make the cars competitive in 1984.

3: 1984: First Double World Championship

What was to emerge from McLaren International was not only the year's most successful car, the MP4/2, but one of the best organized teams that has ever competed in Formula 1. John Barnard, following a policy of careful and thoughtful evolution, redesigned the monocoque of the 1983 car to accommodate the TAG engine, which was shorter than its Cosworth predecessor, and to take account of the fact that there was a 220-litre fuel limit in 1984 and a ban on refuelling – so there was no question of running an undersized tank. The monocoque featured a longer, lower section behind the cockpit to house the fuel bag, the lower sides of the chassis flared outwards so as to improve airflow into the side pods and there was a pronounced curve at the rear of each pod revealing horizontal fins formed by the undertray, a narrow tail shroud and either side of this a wide diffuser passing through the rear suspension. For driver protection there was an aluminium nose-box which housed the front coil spring/damper units. Distinguishing the cars from their 1983 predecessors were the large rear wings with three-piece winglets.

As on the MP4/1 cars the front suspension by push-rods, rockers and lower wishbones was retained, but although the general suspension layout at the rear was similar, with wide-based flat-section lower wishbones, fabricated upper rocking arms and inboard coil spring/damper units, because of the shorter engine it was possible to move the coil spring/damper mountings further forward and the rocker arms raked back.

By 1984 the design of the TAG P01 engine had been settled and the power output on race boost was now 750 bhp at 11,500 rpm, comparable with that of Renault, but rather less powerful than the BMW engine powering the Brabhams. One of the major problems with the early engines had been the shortcomings of the Bosch Motronic engine management system and the failure of the alternator had also been a major problem, eliminating Lauda at Monza and at Kyalami in 1983. Hard work by Bosch, who had very limited racing experience, eventually resolved this problem and the Motronic management system was to play a major role in the success of the TAG engine. Porsche were able to comply with McLaren's requirements that they needed 15 race engines together with at least five extra sets of components by June 1984. At this stage the McLarens, unusually, still retained onboard starter motors.

The one weak area of the McLaren in 1984 was the transmission which was still a McLaren-evolved gearbox with mainly Hewland internals, not really up to coping with the power of the TAG engine.

In all only four MP4/2s were completed in 1984, although the team also had a spare monocoque. Chassis MP4/2-4 was completed in mid-season, but was retained by the McLaren test team and was never raced.

Niki Lauda remained with the team, but McLaren secured the services of Alain Prost who had been sacked by Renault after coming so close to winning the 1983 World Championship. Prost had previously driven for McLaren in 1980. Lauda remained with the team and this meant that Watson was dropped, bringing an end to his Formula 1 career.

Brazilian Grand Prix

Prior to the race held on the Rio Janeiro Autodrome there had been very little chance to test the new McLarens, apart from a brief session at the Paul Ricard circuit. Although troublefree in practice, neither Lauda nor Prost could quite match the speed of the front runners and de Angelis (Lotus 95T-Renault) took pole position in 1m 28.392s with Prost fourth fastest in 1m 29.330s and Lauda sixth in 1m 29.854s.

The race was run in very hot and dry conditions and many of the teams were worried about fuel consumption. Although Alboreto (Ferrari) led initially from Warwick (Renault), Lauda came through to take the lead on lap 12 and by lap 24 Prost was up into second place. The two McLarens held station until lap 38 when Lauda failed to appear, Prost came into the pits for new tyres (a delayed stop because of a jammed rear wheel nut) and Lauda trailed in behind to retire with electrical problems. Prost rejoined the race in second place behind Warwick who seemed all set for a victory when his Renault's left-front upper wishbone broke and Prost scored an unexpected win ahead of Rosberg's Williams. It is also significant that Prost had set fastest lap of the race at 116.622 mph.

Lauda's MP4/2 in the pit lane at Kyalami in 1984.

South African Grand Prix

In practice at Kyalami McLaren battled with problems with the Bosch Motronic engine management system, quite possibly because of the high altitude of the circuit (5300 feet), the engines were picking up roughly out of slow corners and misfiring badly between 7000 and 8000 rpm. During Friday afternoon's qualifying Prost used the spare car, MP4/2-3, which was fitted with smaller turbochargers than the race cars, and he found not only improved throttle response but sufficient speed to give him fifth place on the grid in 1m 05.354s. Lauda was eighth fastest in 1m 06.043s. It was decided that both drivers would run in the race with the smaller turbochargers. Pole position at Kyalami went to Piquet with the turbocharged Brabham-BMW, exploiting to the full his special qualifying engine to record 1m 04.871s.

During the warm-up on race morning Lauda's TAG engine was misfiring badly. Luckily for McLaren, the warm-up was halted because of a serious accident to Ghinzani (Osella) and this gave the team time to sort out the problem and Lauda set second fastest time. More problems followed when Prost's McLaren refused to start on the grid for the final parade lap because the fuel pump drive had failed. Because of Lauda's earlier problem, the spare car sat fuelled and kitted out to suit the Austrian. The mechanics swiftly swapped components on the spare to suit Prost who, waved on to the track by a marshal, accelerated away after the field which was now forming up on the grid. Racing regulations stated that Prost should start from the pit lane, but fortunately for McLaren, the start was delayed because two drivers had stalled near the back of the grid and the team immediately repositioned correctly Prost in the pit lane so that he could start from there.

While Lauda held fourth place, Prost was fighting his way through the field. Rosberg (Williams) led initially, but soon Piquet had brought his Brabham to the front and Fabi moved up into second place with the second of the BMW-powered cars. Lauda passed Rosberg's ill-handling Williams on lap 4, six laps later he was in second place and he took the lead on lap 20 when Piquet pulled into the pits for fresh tyres.

The South African race established the supremacy of McLaren. Here is Prost who finished second, just over a minute behind his team-mate.

Both Piquet and Fabi retired and so Lauda now led Rosberg by the comfortable margin of 40 seconds. By lap 43 Prost had worked his way through to second place, about 30 seconds behind Lauda and the two McLaren drivers retained their positions until the chequered flag. Derek Warwick brought his Renault across the line in third place, a lap in arrears, ahead of Patrese (Alfa Romeo), de Cesaris (Ligier) and Senna (Toleman).

Belgian Grand Prix

The Belgian Grand Prix at Zolder brought problems for McLaren in both practice and in the race. During Saturday afternoon's qualifying Prost spun three times because the Motronic management system was causing the engine to cut in and out and he had to rely on his Friday's time, eighth place on the grid in 1m 16.72s. During Friday's qualifying Lauda's car developed a fuel leak which resulted in a fire and he was forced to abandon the car out on the circuit. He lost 45 minutes of Saturday's qualifying because of a faulty coil, he then suffered final drive problems and the spare car had a sticking fuel pressure relief valve. The result was that he had only 15 minutes of practice and could manage no better than 14th place in 1m 18.071s. At this race the Ferraris had shown remarkable form and Alboreto and Arnoux took first two places on the grid (Alboreto's pole position time was 1m 14.846s).

Alboreto led throughout the race and both the McLarens ran into problems. Prost retired on lap 6 because of a broken distributor rotor; Lauda was slowed by a cracked intercooler that resulted in a loss of boost pressure, dropping back to 12th place, and retired on lap 36 when the water pump failed. It was to prove McLaren's worst showing of the year.

San Marino Grand Prix

Wet weather marred much of practice for the San Marino Grand Prix. Friday afternoon's qualifying was very wet to begin with, but the circuit gradually

Niki Lauda with the MP4/2 in the pits at the Belgian Grand Prix.

dried out. During this session Prost found his MP4/2 running roughly and switched to the spare car which he decided to retain for the race. During Saturday afternoon's qualifying, on a damp track that gradually dried out, Prost turned in a lap in 1m 28.628s, good enough for second place on the grid behind Piquet (1m 28.51s), whilst Lauda was back on the third row with a time of 1m 30.325s.

Prost made a brilliant start in the race, accelerating straight into the lead as the lights turned green and he stayed in front for the full 60 laps – despite a spin on lap 23, from which he successfully recovered and as he passed the pits he tapped the side of his helmet in self-criticism. Later testing revealed that the problem was a faulty master cylinder that could jam without warning. Prost stopped to change tyres at the end of lap 30 and at the end of the race he led Arnoux's Ferrari by a margin of a little over 13 seconds. For Lauda it was another disappointing race, for he made a poor start because of difficulty in getting his car into first gear, and as he accelerated away he was forced to lift off to avoid Rosberg's stalled Williams. As the race progressed, so Lauda began to climb up through the field from tenth place at the end of lap 1. On lap 12 he passed Alboreto's Ferrari, was repassed, but neatly slipped ahead again to take fifth place, and he passed Arnoux's Ferrari on the next lap. Lauda then closed on Warwick's Renault, looking for a chance to overtake, but on lap 16 the Austrian's McLaren was eliminated by piston failure. Prost now led the World Championship with 24 points to the 13 of Derek Warwick and with Lauda in fifth equal place with 9 points.

French Grand Prix

During qualifying at the Dijon circuit the McLarens were plagued by engine failures and in all three TAG engines blew up because of piston failure. To say the team was worried, would be to express it mildly, and as a result of these problems Prost was in fifth place on the grid with a time of 1m 02.982s. Lauda was ninth fastest in 1m 04.419s. Pole position went to Tambay (Renault) with a time of

Lauda during Friday's damp practice session at Imola for the 1984 San Marino Grand Prix.

At Imola Alain Prost was second fastest in practice to Piquet's Brabham and led throughout this 60-lap race.

1m 02.200s. All the fastest times were set on the Friday, because Saturday's qualifying was wet. Because of the engine problems, Porsche had rushed to the circuit two revised engines on the Saturday evening and they were installed that night. Once the engines had been installed, it was discovered that Prost's car suffered from a serious misfire and it took four hours for this to be cured.

The McLaren team faced the race with some trepidation, because Prost had found that his car was running rough between 8000 and 9000 rpm during the warm-up and of course there was no guarantee that Porsche had solved the engine problem. At the end of the first lap Prost was in seventh place and Lauda ninth. By lap 18 Prost was second behind Tambay (Renault) and three laps later Lauda moved up to hold third position. Five laps later Prost's McLaren suddenly veered to the left on the fast Pouas curve. The left-front wheel had worked loose and Prost was lucky to escape a very bad accident only because the wheel jammed against the brake caliper. The Frenchman pulled across to the right of the track and made his way slowly to the pits. Despite exhaustive tests later, no good reason was found why the retaining nut should have parted company with the wheel. Prost's pit stop was lengthy and he rejoined the race in 11th place. Lauda closed up on

Top Left: Ron Dennis, head of McLaren International, and one of the most successful racing managers of all time.

Top Right: One of the longest serving McLaren drivers was John Watson who joined the team for 1979 and was dropped at the end of 1983, bringing his Formula 1 career effectively to a conclusion.

1983

Left: Niki Lauda, one of the most experienced and one of the most able of all Formula 1 drivers, joined McLaren for 1984 and soon settled down with the new TAG-turbocharged cars.

Below: The Porsche-designed and built TAG turbocharged engine installed in the MP4/1E 'interim' chassis.

Right: The turbocharged MP4/1E first appeared at the 1983 Dutch Grand Prix where it was driven by Niki Lauda. Lauda and the McLaren are seen in the pits.

Above: Lauda with the MP4/1E in practice for the 1983 Dutch Grand Prix. He retired in the race because of brake problems.

Alain Prost who joined McLaren for 1984 and stayed with the team until the end of the 1989 season when he left to drive for Ferrari.

1984

Prost with his winning MP4/2 in the 1984 Brazilian Grand Prix at Rio de Janeiro.

Above: Niki Lauda in the 1984 Belgian Grand Prix in which he retired because of water pump failure.

Right: Alain Prost in the pits at the 1984 San Marino Grand Prix at Imola. He led throughout the race.

Saturday's qualifying at the French Grand Prix at Dijon was marred by cool, wet weather. Here Prost splashes round with the MP4/2.

At Dijon Niki Lauda was in fine form, despite practice problems, and came through to win the race from Tambay's Renault.

Motor racing at its most miserable: Alain Prost in the wet 1984 Monaco Grand Prix which was stopped after 31 laps – just as he was about to be passed by Senna's Toleman.

Niki Lauda in practice for the 1984 Canadian Grand Prix in which he took second place behind Nelson Piquet (Brabham BT53-BMW).

Niki Lauda, winner of the 1984 British Grand Prix at Brands Hatch, at the wheel of his MP4/2.

Right: In the Austrian Grand Prix Niki Lauda scored his fourth race victory of the year and consolidated his lead in the World Championship.

Below: Piquet and the Brabham BT53, the fieriest driver and the fastest car, posed a constant threat to McLaren in 1984.

Work on the MP4/2s alongside the team transporter in the paddock at the French Grand Prix at Dijon.

Tambay, who was far from happy with his brakes, and slipped into the lead on lap 41. When Lauda made his routine pit stop for new tyres, he had a lead of 30 seconds, but the stop took longer than expected and he rejoined the race 11 seconds behind Tambay. Within a mere eight laps however, he had regained the lead and at the finish he was a comfortable 8 seconds ahead of the Renault. After a rousing drive through the field, Prost finished seventh, a lap in arrears.

Niki Lauda on the victory podium at Dijon flanked by Tambay (on his right) and Mansell.

Monaco Grand Prix

So far during the season few changes had been made to the McLarens, but at Monaco the cars appeared with new Gleason-type differentials and new and specially developed lightweight turbocharger housings from KKK. The McLarens were completely troublefree in practice, Prost was third fastest in the first practice session on the Thursday afternoon and took pole position on the Saturday afternoon in 1m 22.661s. Lauda's performance was disappointing, partly because he had been baulked by Baldi's Spirit when running on his second set of qualifying tyres during the final session and he took eighth place on the grid in 1m 23.886s.

After the beautiful warm dry weather that had characterised the qualifying sessions, the most familiar aspect of Monaco weather, race day revealed

Alain Prost on his way to a narrow victory in the rain-soaked Monaco Grand Prix leads Laffite's Williams.

the other side of Monaco's weather pattern, torrential rain and low cloud that masked the heights of the cliffs. It was only too obvious that there would be no relenting of these conditions during the day. In an effort to make the circuit uniformly wet throughout, a water tanker soaked the tunnel section of the circuit beneath the Loews Hotel, but the only effect of this was to delay the start, for within just a few laps a dry line had emerged. When the green light came on, Prost gently nosed ahead and settled down to lead at a steady pace, whilst all the drivers behind him had to battle with great clouds of spray. At the end of the fifth lap Lauda was in fifth place, but he had soon moved up to third ahead of the two Ferraris. On lap 11 as Prost exited from Portier and accelerated towards the tunnel, he was confronted by Corrado Fabi's Brabham stationary on the track, Prost aimed for the narrow gap unfortunately striking a marshal who was trying to move the Brabham. In the confusion that followed, Nigel Mansell was able to push through into the lead with his Lotus 95T. Mansell's lead was short-lived for five laps later, driving unnecessarily fast in the conditions, he lost control on the white road markings as he climbed from St. Devote and hit the guard rails. Lauda had reached second place, but he spun out of the race on lap 24 at the entry to Casino Square. It seemed that the rain was falling even heavier and in these appalling conditions Senna (Toleman) and Bellof (Tyrrell) began to close up on the leading McLaren. However, Clerk of the Course Jacky Ickx had decided that enough was enough and the red flag was hung out at the end of lap 32 just as Senna was about to pass Prost. The result stood as at the end of lap 31, with Prost the winner, Senna second and Bellof third.

Canadian Grand Prix

The teams now travelled to the west of the Atlantic for the three races on the North American continent. At the Gilles Villeneuve circuit at Montreal the Brabham team which had been out of luck all

Nelson Piquet completely dominated the Canadian Grand Prix with his Brabham, taking pole position, leading throughout and setting fastest lap.

season so far, showed superb form and Nelson Piquet, the 1983 World Champion, took pole position in 1m 25.442s, with Prost second fastest in 1m 26.198s. The McLarens had not been without their problems in practice, although Prost had set fastest lap in Friday's qualifying. During that session he had spun at the last corner because his carbon-fibre brakes were running too hot and he also suffered engine failure on the Saturday. He then went out in Lauda's car, with his second set of qualifying tyres, but he was quite unable to match Piquet's time. Lauda could manage no better than eighth place on the grid behind Nigel Mansell's Lotus.

The race represented a magnificent display of power and control by Piquet and the Brabham team. Initially Piquet led from Prost, but it soon became evident that Prost's engine was down on power and not picking up cleanly, so Piquet was able to maintain a steady pace, conserving his brakes while running with full tanks. As the race progressed so Lauda worked his way up through the field, moving up into third place by lap 14 and going ahead of his team-mate on lap 44. Despite a very painful right foot (after the race it was discovered to be very badly blistered) and the temptation to stop at the pits, Piquet drove a programmed race to finish the 70 laps two and a half seconds ahead of Lauda. The winner, Lauda and Prost were the only drivers to finish the full 70 laps. Fourth-place man de Angelis with the Lotus was a lap in arrears. After the race Lauda freely admitted that his car simply lacked the power to match the Brabham's speed.

The McLarens held second and third places for most of the Canadian race and Lauda finished second, 2½ seconds behind the winner.

United States Grand Prix (Detroit)

The Grand Prix circus moved on to the very difficult and tortuous 2.50-mile Detroit circuit, bumpy, lined by concrete walls and with few run-off areas, in one of the more depressing parts of this sprawling city and in the shadow of the 70-storey Renaissance Centre. Once again Piquet dominated practice and took pole position in 1m 40.980s and once again he was to lead the race throughout, although not without a major problem at the start.

After the Canadian race Prost had complained that his engine was down on power, but at Detroit he still had the same power unit and was far from happy. Prost's main complaint was about throttle lag, but even when the engine had been fitted with new turbochargers he was still unhappy and took second position on the grid in 1m 4.640s with the spare car. Lauda's Friday time was disallowed because the scrutineers had found that the maximum width of his rear aerofoil exceeded the permitted limit by one millimetre. It appears that the problem was caused by heat distorting the bond between the main aerofoil and the side plate. A number of other measurements had been taken and they had revealed the aerofoil to be perfectly legal in all other respects. In Saturday's qualifying Lauda had difficulty in finding a gap in the traffic and ended up in tenth place on the grid with a time of 1m 43.484s.

When the green light came on, Mansell powered through from the second row with his Lotus, believing there was a sufficient gap between Prost's McLaren and Piquet's Brabham and while Prost accelerated away into the lead, the Lotus collided with the Brabham swinging it into Alboreto's Ferrari and then into the retaining wall. The race was stopped and Mansell was subsequently fined $6000 by FISA for dangerous driving.

When the race was restarted, Piquet took the lead ahead of Prost and at the end of the first lap Lauda was in eighth position. Prost was far from happy with the loss of grip of his Michelin tyres and on lap 10 Mansell was able to slip through to take second place. After a pit stop for new tyres Prost began to work his way back through the field, but on

Sole McLaren finisher at Detroit was Prost who took fifth place in another Brabham-dominated race.

lap 39 a rear tyre deflated, Prost kept the engine running as he spun and made a second stop for tyres. Lauda also made a stop for new tyres, but with 33 laps completed he came into the pits because the engine was running roughly. Lauda went out again to form an assessment as to whether or not the team should change the engine prior to practice at Dallas, the next race, and the car was then retired. Piquet won the race from Martin Brundle, who had been well able to exploit his Cosworth-powered Tyrrell on this slow circuit, de Angelis (Lotus) and Fabi (Brabham). Prost took fifth place. At this circuit both cars broke their front anti-roll bars because of the bumpy nature of the circuit. Replacement anti-roll bars in titanium were ordered, but in the meanwhile the cars had to run with heavier-gauge bars.

United States Grand Prix (Dallas)

There were many complaints about Dallas, but the drivers' main worries concerned the bumpy characteristics of the circuit, the lack of run-off areas and the concrete walls. Fastest in practice was Mansell who lapped in 1m 37.041s, with de Angelis second in 1m 37.635s and it was clear that the Lotus 95Ts were more competitive on this circuit than most in 1984. Lauda was fifth fastest in 1m 37.987s, but during qualifying he hit the retaining walls twice, damaging the suspension of both his race car and team's spare. Prost was two places slower in 1m 38.544s. Mansell and de Angelis led initially in the race, but the winner was Keke Rosberg with his Williams-Honda and with René Arnoux in second place. Both McLarens were eliminated by collisions with retaining walls.

British Grand Prix

Unofficial practice at Brands Hatch was delayed for more than an hour, following a very bad accident; Venezuelan driver Johnny Cecotto lost his Toleman on the dusty surface and slammed into the guard-rail, suffering severe leg and ankle injuries. It was a case of going too fast too soon before a racing line had developed on the track. The McLarens dominated Friday's qualifying, whereas Piquet was in trouble with his Brabham. However, on the Saturday Piquet took pole position in 1m 10.869s, with Prost second in 1m 11.076s and Lauda third fastest in 1m 11.344s.

Initially Piquet led the race, with Prost second, de Angelis third, but with Lauda moving up into third place on lap 2. On lap 11 Palmer's RAM broke its steering and hit the tyre barriers on the outside of Clearways. Because the car was considered to be in a dangerous position, the red flag was displayed at the end of lap 12, but the leaders had already started lap 13 and in accordance with the rules at the re-start the cars formed up on the grid in the order that they had finished lap 11. This caused something of an upset, because Piquet had pulled into the pits at the end of lap 11 so though he was actually back in third

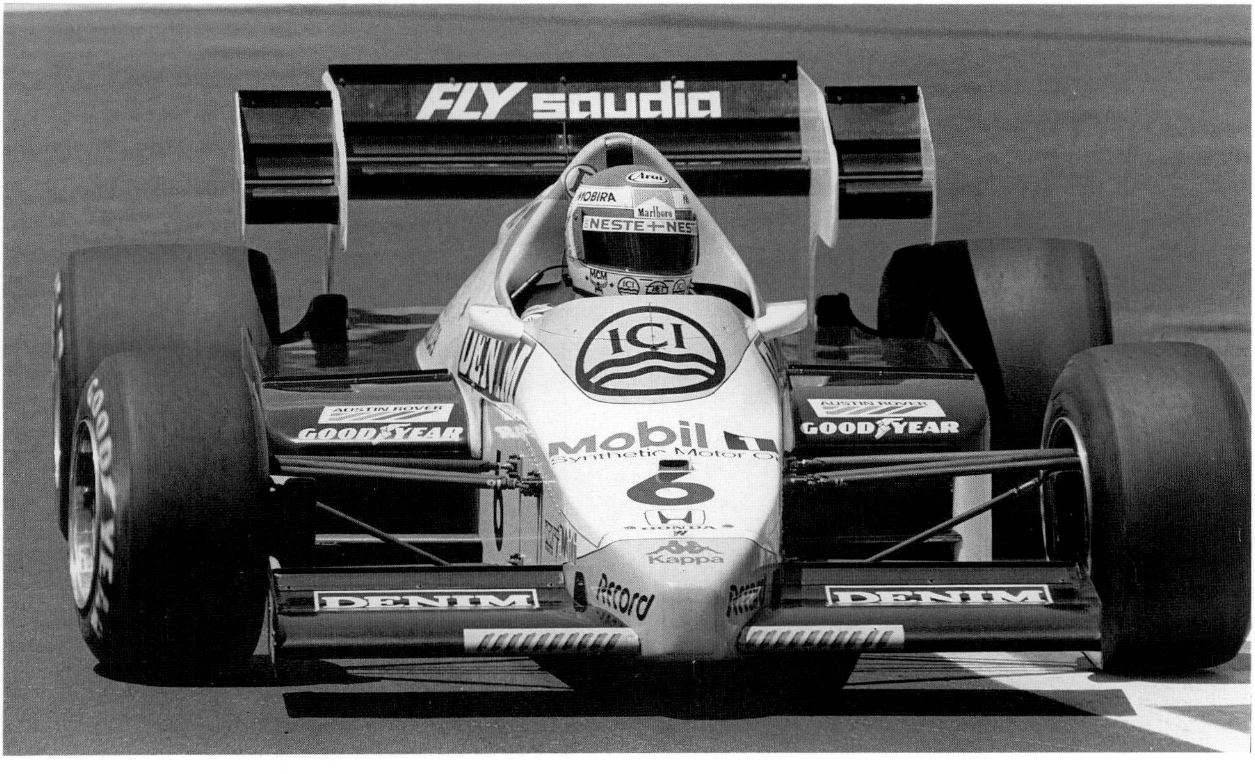

Keke Rosberg winner of the 1984 United States Grand Prix (Dallas) with his Honda-powered Williams FW09.

Niki Lauda won the British Grand Prix at Brands Hatch. With this success under his belt he was second in the World Championship, 1½ points behind team-mate Prost.

place at the start of lap 13, he took pole position on the new grid. When the race restarted, Prost went straight into the lead ahead of Piquet with Lauda third. Lauda took second place from Piquet on lap 17 and it looked as though a fine dice was going to build up between the two leading McLarens, as Prost fought hard to maintain an advantage over Lauda. For once Prost had been trying just a little too hard, for he slowed on lap 27 and cruised back to the pits to retire with the McLaren's Achilles' heel, gearbox problems. Piquet closed up on Lauda, and it seemed as though the Brazilian was going to fight for the lead, but because of a fluctuating turbocharger boost pressure he gradually fell back and at the finish Lauda led Warwick's Renault by a little over 40 seconds. After this race Prost still led the World Championship with 34.5 points (half points were awarded at Monaco) but Lauda was close behind him with 33 points.

German Grand Prix

By the Hockenheim race Formula 1 had settled into a pattern of McLaren domination, disrupted only by the fiery driving and sheer power of the Piquet/Brabham opposition. Prost took pole position in 1m 47.012s, with Piquet fifth fastest in 1m 48.584s, mainly because he had been baulked by Mansell and de Cesaris on the Saturday, and Lauda took seventh place on the grid in 1m 48.192s.

Because of fuel pump problems on the Sunday morning, Prost switched to the spare car. By error the organisers had set out the starting grid incorrectly so that Prost in pole position was on the outside, whereas his position should have been on the inside of the circuit. The result was that de Angelis took the lead initially, with Prost chopping Warwick for second place and Piquet rapidly moving up into third spot. Prost closed on de Angelis, the Italian was weaving along the straight to hold Prost off and on lap 8 the turbocharger of de Angelis's Renault engine blew; as the Lotus slowed, so Prost lifted off and Piquet took the opportunity to grab the lead. As the race progressed, Piquet extended his lead to 5.6 seconds and Lauda moved up into third place. On lap 20 Piquet dropped back to third place and at the end of the next lap pulled into the pits to retire with gearbox problems. Prost was determined to extend his lead in the World Championship, gradually pulling away from Lauda, setting fastest lap, and at the end of this 44-lap race he was just over three seconds ahead of his team mate. Warwick (Renault) finished third ahead of Mansell's Lotus.

Austrian Grand Prix

Once again Piquet took pole position at the Österreichring in 1m 26.173s, with Prost in second place in 1m 26.203s. De Angelis was third fastest with his Lotus in 1m 26.318s and Lauda was fourth fastest with a time of 1m 26.715s. At the start, Derek Ongaro pressed the button to turn the starting lights green, but saw that both de Angelis and Rothengatter (Spirit) were holding up their hands to indicate that they had stalled. Immediately Ongaro pushed the button to switch on flashing orange lights, but because of an electrical problem the green light was shown briefly and half the grid moved off. The race was stopped and restarted. Although Prost was away first, Piquet had soon forced his way into the lead and Lauda was in sixth place, moving steadily towards the front. Already Prost had gearbox troubles and for much of each lap was having to hold the McLaren in fourth, steering with one hand. On lap 28 the Renault engine of de Angelis's Lotus, in fourth place, blew its turbocharger and the Italian started to crawl back to the pits. The marshals were slow to display the oil flags, Piquet almost lost control of the Brabham and Prost, steering with one hand, spun off the circuit with a stalled engine. Already Lauda had moved up into third place and he was now second behind the Brabham. As Piquet's tyres deteriorated so his efforts to hold off Lauda became increasingly doomed and on lap 39 Lauda slipped into the lead. Despite the loss of fourth gear three laps later, accompanied by an explosive bang as a ring-tooth hit the inside of the gearbox casing, Lauda carried on to win by just over 24 seconds from Piquet, with Alboreto (Ferrari) third and Fabi (Brabham) fourth.

Dutch Grand Prix

Another of the few changes made to the cars during the year was seen at Zandvoort where they appeared with enlarged square turbocharger air intakes on the sides of the rear bodywork. Alain Prost took pole position in 1m 13.567s, and Nelson Piquet with the Brabham was second fastest in 1m 13.872s. An engine down on power and then a spin frustrated the Brazilian's efforts at taking pole position. Lauda was in sixth place on the grid in 1m 14.866s.

Piquet made a brilliant start when the lights turned green, Prost was second, but Lauda was slow off the line and at the end of the first lap was in ninth place. After ten laps, during which he laid a fine spray of oil, Piquet retired with no oil pressure and now Prost led from Rosberg (Williams) and Lauda was up into third place. Soon Lauda passed Rosberg and Prost found his team-mate rapidly closing. At the chequered flag Prost was ten seconds ahead of Lauda, and Mansell and de Angelis finished third and fourth with their Renault-powered Lotus 95Ts. Lauda's lead in the World Championship had narrowed to 1½ points (54 to Prost's 52.5).

Italian Grand Prix

Once again at Monza Piquet took pole position on the grid, with a lap in 1m 26.584s, but Prost, who had switched to his spare car on the Saturday

Prost's MP4/2 in the pits at the 1984 Dutch Grand Prix at Zandvoort.

Alain Prost's win at Zandvoort was McLaren's ninth in 1984, beating the record set by Lotus in 1978 and he was now back in close contention for the World Championship with 52.5 points to the 54 of Lauda.

after engine problems with his race car, was second on the grid in 1m 26.671s. Lauda was fourth fastest in 1m 28.533s. During qualifying Niki Lauda suffered a slipped disc, and although it looked as though he might have to miss the race, massage and a good night's rest meant that he made the start.

At the start de Angelis narrowly accelerated into the lead, but then Piquet's Brabham thrust ahead pulling away from Prost who led Tambay (Renault), de Angelis, Fabi (Brabham) and Lauda. With only three laps completed, Prost was out of the race because of turbocharger failure and Lauda eased his pace to secure World Championship points, rather than win. Piquet had damaged his Brabham's water radiator when clipping a kerb, the engine lost its coolant and the BMW-powered car slowed off at the end of lap 15 and retired a lap later. Tambay now led from Fabi and Lauda, with Lauda struggling hard to pass the second Brabham driver and not succeeding until lap 42 on the straight leading to the Parabolica. He took Tambay, slowed by throttle problems on the next lap, both Fabi and Tambay retired and at the end of this 51-lap race Lauda led Alboreto (Ferrari) across the line by the comfortable margin of over 24 seconds.

European Grand Prix

In 1984 there was a second race in Germany, at the newly rebuilt and totally emasculated Nürburgring. Almost inevitably Piquet was the dominant force in practice and took pole position in 1m 18.871s, with Prost in second place in 1m 19.175s. Lauda's qualifying was full of problems. With the spare car he came to a halt on his first lap on the Friday because of a wiring problem. He then took out his race car, only to stop again because of oil leaking into the clutch from the gearbox. When rain began to fall, Lauda's prospects of a good time were gone and he finished the day in 15th place on the grid. Any hope of improving during Saturday's qualifying were literally washed out by rain throughout the qualifying session. On the Sunday morning Prost slid on to a kerb, and spun across the grass into a parked car, breaking a wheel. Whether that was all the damage that there was, it was difficult to assess, so the mechanics immediately started work changing components and also replaced the engine that had been leaking water.

Piquet made a slow start and Prost accelerated

When Prost scored his sixth victory of the season in the European Grand Prix at the newly rebuilt Nürburgring, he was still very much in contention for the World Championship.

away into a lead that he maintained throughout the 67 laps of this race. By lap 22 Lauda was in sixth place, Alboreto passed Baldi's Spirit on the inside at the last corner before the start/finish line and Lauda went through after him. The rear brakes of the McLaren locked, Lauda spun wildly through 360 degrees, keeping his engine running and accelerating away without losing a place. He had however, flat-spotted his tyres and they deteriorated badly as the race progressed. On the last lap Piquet, who had been in second place for many laps, ran out of fuel, was passed by Alboreto (Ferrari) and so the finishing order was Prost-Alboreto-Piquet-Lauda.

Portuguese Grand Prix

The Portuguese race was held on the new 2.703-mile Estoril circuit and there had been a frantic rush to get the circuit ready in time for the race. Once again Piquet took pole position in practice in 1m 21.703s, with Prost second fastest in 1m 21.774s and after engine problems on the Friday Lauda was back in 11th place on the grid with a time of 1m 23.183s. Although both Prost and Lauda approached the conflict that would settle the World Championship with stoic calm, the press hyped the situation beyond all reason. Prost was away first when the lights turned green, Rosberg accelerated down the outside from the left hand side of the second row of the grid and at the end of the first lap the Finnish driver's Williams led from Mansell (Lotus) and Prost, with Lauda back in 11th place. Piquet spun on the first lap and resumed the race at the tail of the field.

On the second lap Prost nipped into second place when Mansell slid wide at a tight left-hand corner, but it was not until lap 9 that Prost assumed the lead at the end of the start/finish straight. As had happened so often in 1984, Lauda steadily progressed through the field, passing Cheever (Renault) on lap 3, Tambay on lap 5 and whilst he had difficulty in overtaking Johansson's Toleman he eventually managed to get ahead on lap 28, clouting the Hart-powered car's nose as he went by. Lauda was now in fifth place, two laps later he overtook Rosberg's Williams, after another two laps he had passed Senna's Toleman and he was second behind his McLaren team-mate on lap 52 after Mansell had spun away his second place because of brake failure. At the finish Lauda was a little over 13 seconds behind Prost who took the World Championship with 72 points to Prost's 71.5 points.

The year 1984 was for McLaren the beginning of a long period of Formula 1 domination. During 1984 the team had won 12 of the year's 16 races (seven to Prost and five to Lauda), McLaren had won

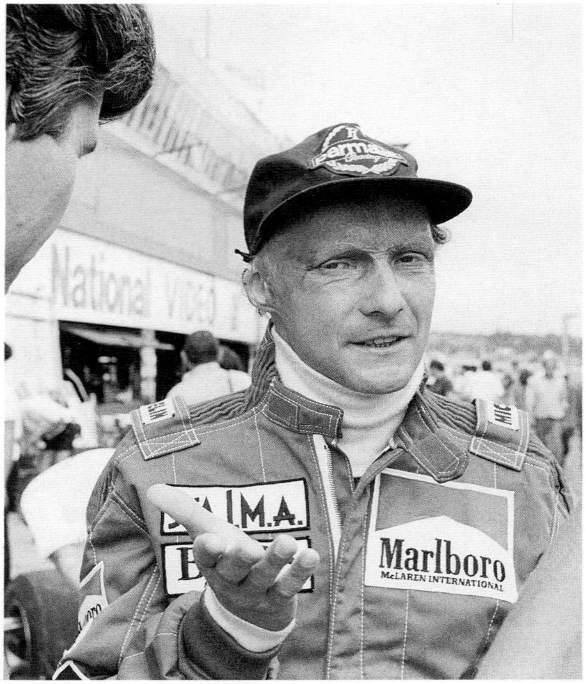

Niki Lauda, 1984 World Champion, with 72 points.

Alain Prost, second in the 1984 World Championship, with 71.5 points.

the Constructors' Cup by a monumental margin (143.5 points to the 57.5 of Ferrari) and had set fastest lap at eight of the year's races (five by Lauda and three by Prost). Undoubtedly Piquet's Brabham had been faster both in qualifying and in the early stages of most races (the Brazilian had taken nine pole positions during the year), but Brabham's reliability had been sadly lacking. The only other real opposition during the year had come from Lotus who occasionally got to grips with the McLarens, but failed to win a single race (Piquet won two for Brabham and one victory each was scored by Williams and Ferrari) and Lotus could count as little more than the best of the also-rans.

4: *1985: World Championship Repeat*

With the now established pattern of 16 races in a year, plus testing sessions, the interval in time between the last race of 1984, the Portuguese Grand Prix on 21 October, and the first race of 1985, the Brazilian Grand Prix, was five months. This was longer than in many other years, but the time for development and testing of new cars was desperately short for all the leading teams.

For 1985 John Barnard produced the MP4/2B, a clear descendant of the very successful line of cars that had first appeared in 1981. McLaren raced five chassis in 1984, but only two were new and three were updated 1984 cars. The main differences in 1985 were that the monocoque had to be revised to comply with new nose box regulations, resulting in a longer and sleeker nose. There was a smaller rear wing, again necessary to comply with a change in the regulations and the side pods were shorter and the rear bodywork narrower; at the front there were new suspension uprights and there was a new push-rod suspension system at the rear. McLaren had finally abandoned the trans-axle which had powered all the MP4 series of cars and now used a new and much slimmer trans-axle case, although the same internals were retained, including gears made specially for the team by EMCO of Chicago from 1984 onwards. Because of problems of grease leakage from the constant-velocity joints, McLaren adopted a new arrangement that incorporated the joints with the rear hubs and used ball instead of taper bearings.

Porsche had been continuing, with considerable success, development work on the TAG turbocharged engine. Power output was increased, the water losses that the TAG engines had suffered from in 1984 were cured and the Bosch Motronic engine management system was now so efficient and effective that the team could calculate with great accuracy the fuel load needed for a race, and thereby avoiding carrying extra fuel and extra weight. Michelin had now withdrawn from racing, so McLaren was forced to switch to Goodyear tyres – the only other manufacturer in racing was Pirelli. It was soon discovered that the Goodyears proved less durable, so that there were problems of grip, initially at the rear, but the situation changed, so that later in the year the MP4/2Bs suffered lack of front-end grip.

McLaren's main rivals in 1985 proved to be Ferrari, Lotus and Williams, together with Brabham, all of whom won races during the year.

Brazilian Grand Prix

Prior to Rio de Janeiro, the only appearance of the MP4/2B had been at a brief test session in the wet at Brands Hatch. Both Alain Prost and Niki Lauda were well satisfied with the new cars and reckoned that they were a considerable improvement over the 1984 MP4/2s. The team did however recognise that development work was needed to improve the handling on slower corners. Both drivers were plagued by minor problems in practice. Prost was back in sixth place in 1m 29.117s whilst Lauda was two rows further back on the grid with a time of 1m 29.984s. Michele Alboreto (Ferrari) took pole position in 1m 27.768s, displaying only too clearly the great strides in development that Maranello had made over the winter months.

At the start Mansell (Williams) and Alboreto collided. The British car was eliminated, but Mansell's team-mate, Rosberg, pulled away from the rest of the field with Alboreto second, Prost third, and Lauda eighth. Rosberg retired on lap 9 with turbocharger failure. Prost was right up the exhausts of Alboreto, whose steering geometry had been damaged in the collision with Mansell and on lap 19 when the Ferrari driver missed a gear, Prost swooped into the lead and remained in front for the remaining 43 laps to win by just over 3 seconds from Alboreto, with de Angelis (Lotus) in third place, a lap in arrears. Lauda retired at the end of lap 23 because of failure of the fuel metering unit, although he did rejoin the race again briefly to check whether the problem had been cured. This was McLaren's eighth successive Championship race victory.

Alain Prost in practice for the 1985 Brazilian Grand Prix at Rio de Janeiro with the new MP4/2B car. Although he had turbocharger problems in practice, he came through to win the race comfortably from Alboreto's Ferrari.

Portuguese Grand Prix

Ayrton Senna (Lotus-Renault) dominated practice at Estoril and took pole position in 1m 21.007s, the first pole position in his career. Prost was second on the grid in 1m 21.420s, but Lauda was back on the fourth row with a time of 1m 23.288s, after having to switch to the spare during Saturday's dry practice. His own car had gear-selection trouble and Lauda was far from happy with the handling of the team spare.

Shortly before the start of the race on the Sunday, torrential rain began to fall and in these conditions Senna took the lead which he retained throughout this race, shortened because of the bad weather, from 69 laps to 67 to comply with the two-hour rule. For much of the race his team-mate de Angelis held second place behind him, with Prost third and Lauda climbing up to hold fourth place. When the rain was at its very worst, Prost hit a deep puddle on the start-finish straight, spun violently and clouted the barrier with his rear wing. Not long afterwards, Lauda retired his MP4/2B with engine failure. Behind Senna the finishing order was Alboreto (Ferrari), Tambay (Renault) and de Angelis who had slowed during the later laps of the race.

San Marino Grand Prix

At the Imola race, practice was dominated by the opposition, with Senna taking his second pole position in 1m 27.327s, ahead of Rosberg (Williams), de Angelis (Lotus) and Alboreto (Ferrari) with Prost in sixth place in 1m 28.099s, and Lauda eighth in 1m 28.399s. Neither of the McLarens was at its best in practice; Prost had minor brake problems during Friday's qualification. Lauda was forced to stop by a deflated tyre caused by a rear brake caliper scoring through a rim and on the Saturday he also had engine problems which necessitated an engine change and very limited qualifying time. In all the circumstances the positions on the grid were more than acceptable.

Although there was a heavy rain shower before the race, the track had dried out by the start. Early in the race, Prost held fourth place behind Senna, de Angelis and Alboreto and Lauda soon came through to fifth place. Alboreto retired his Ferrari because of electrical problems and de Angelis was passed by both Prost and Lauda. Unfortunately for Lauda, the TAG engine's computer was playing up, causing it to cut in and out and as a result Lauda spun wildly at the chicane leading on to the pit straight; he recovered and carried on, but later he lost fifth gear and was forced to hold fourth in to stop it jumping out. Prost had now closed on Senna and was pushing hard, and whilst the Brazilian was driving with a coolness that was to become characteristic, at this stage in his career it was something remarkable. Senna ran out of fuel on lap 57, three laps from the finish, and Johansson took the lead from Prost and de Angelis. On the next lap Johansson also ran out of fuel and Prost swept by to lead from de Angelis. This was the finishing order, with Boutsen (Arrows) in third place, a lap in arrears. After the race the winning McLaren was found to be two kilogrammes below the minimum weight and so Prost was disqualified. If Prost had pulled up immediately after crossing the finishing line, it is likely that the car would have just about reached the minimum weight level. So de Angelis was the race winner, ahead of Boutsen, Tambay (Renault) and with Niki Lauda fourth.

At Imola Prost drove a well-judged race and was first on the road, but was disqualified because the car was slightly overweight at post-race weighing. This would have been avoided if the weighing station had been manned before the race when McLaren wanted to weigh the car.

Monaco Grand Prix

At Monaco, following testing at Zolder, a number of changes were seen to the McLarens, including a smaller front wing, modified turbochargers and, as a result of the testing, a solution to the electronics problems which had plagued Lauda at both Rio de Janeiro and Imola. Qualifying revealed that Senna was *the* man of the year, and at the third successive race he took pole position on the grid in 1m 20.450s, with Mansell second fastest with his Williams in 1m 20.536s. Already Senna was showing signs of the forcefulness and aggressiveness that were to create problems for him in later years. During the final qualifying session on the Saturday, Senna baulked Lauda so badly that the Austrian later calculatedly forced Senna's Lotus into the escape road at the very tight right-hand corner before the pits. Prost was unhappy with the handling of his car during qualifying and eventually took fifth place on the grid in 1m 20.885s, whilst Lauda was right back on the seventh row with a time of 1m 21.907s.

Senna led away at the start from Mansell, with

Alain Prost on his way to a win in the 1985 Monaco Grand Prix. It was McLaren's second win of the season.

Alboreto third, but quickly moving into second place. On lap 14, Senna retired with engine failure, the result of over-revving during the warm-up when he inadvertently changed from fifth to second. Now Alboreto led from Prost, with de Angelis third and Rosberg (Williams) fourth. Alboreto slid off at St. Devote, but kept his engine running, and Prost took the lead. Six laps later Alboreto was back in front, having passed the McLaren on the inside into St. Devote. Prost's McLaren was plagued by a sticking turbocharger wastegate and it seemed doubtful whether he would be able to stay with the Ferrari driver; on lap 32, however, Alboreto slowed because of a deflating left-rear tyre, made a pit stop for new tyres and rejoined the race in fourth place with Prost firmly in the lead. After being baulked by Patrese's Alfa Romeo for many laps, Lauda eventually got past, but he spun off on lap 18, stalled his engine and was unable to restart. The spin was a result of oil dropped on the road following the collision between the ever-baulking Patrese and Piquet (Brabham). Prost won this 78-lap race from Alboreto (Ferrari) and de Angelis (Lotus).

Canadian Grand Prix

The Belgian Grand Prix should have taken place at Spa-Francorchamps on Sunday, 2 June, but on the Saturday the FISA stewards decided to postpone the race. The reasoning was very simple. A new surface, albeit with excellent drainage qualities, had crumbled badly by the end of the first day's practice. Attempts to repair the surface on the Friday evening had not been adequate and there seemed little alternative but to abandon the event. Although the Formula 1 teams returned to their various bases, a planned Formula 3000 race went ahead and judging by the number of drivers who spun off, it was clear that this race, for somewhat less powerful cars, should not

The 1985 Belgian Grand Prix at Spa-Francorchamps was abandoned because the newly laid surface began to break up. Here is Niki Lauda during qualifying.

have been allowed to go ahead in any event.

Canada was not to prove a McLaren race, and the McLarens seemed well off the pace at the Gilles Villeneuve circuit at Montreal. The Lotus 97Ts of de Angelis and Senna took the first two places on the grid ahead of the Ferraris of Alboreto and Johansson, with Prost fifth fastest in 1m 25.557s. Both McLarens had been plagued by minor problems in qualifying and although Prost's fifth place on the grid was reasonable, Lauda was well back in 17th place in 1m 28.126s, slow throughout qualifying and unhappy with the circuit and car and even – truthfully – complaining in the pits that he had been slowed by a beaver on the circuit.

The race was initially led by the Lotus 97Ts of de Angelis and Senna, but then the Ferraris of Alboreto and Johansson went ahead and Prost, safely ensconced in third place, was prevented from a last corner attempt to pass Johannson when he was baulked by de Cesaris, who was limping round the circuit because of a split brake caliper. Lauda had climbed up to eighth place when he was eliminated by engine overheating.

United States Grand Prix (Detroit)

Once again the Grand Prix teams competed at the depressing, flat, slow Detroit circuit in a race that was to prove a dramatic test of brakes for the McLaren team. Here the MP4/2Bs showed small changes, including different rear suspension set-ups to be tried by both drivers and larger brake cooling ducts. In practice McLaren also used smaller turbochargers. Senna took pole position for the fourth time in 1985 in 1m 42.051s with Mansell (Williams) second fastest in 1m 43.249s. Prost was fourth fastest with his McLaren in 1m 44.088s, despite a crash within a quarter of an hour of the start of practice when brake fluid loss resulted in the rear brakes failing and his McLaren crunching into a tyre barrier. As with all the other leading drivers, his fastest lap was set on the Friday, despite the accident, for Saturday was cool and wet. Lauda could manage no better than 12th fastest in 1m 46.266s.

In the race neither McLaren driver featured in the results, and Prost appeared only on the leader board very briefly. Lauda was in ninth place on lap 11 when his carbon-fibre brakes faded and he was glad to retire. By lap 20 Prost was in seventh place when his brakes faded and, like several other drivers, he crashed at Turn 3. The race was won by Keke Rosberg (Williams) from the Ferraris of Johansson and Alboreto.

French Grand Prix

At the Paul Ricard circuit near Marseille the McLarens appeared with revised front suspension geometry, which largely cured the understeering problem, especially through the slower corners. The team had also now solved the engine problems suffered during qualifying in Belgium and Detroit; these had been caused by fuel and the McLarens were now running on fuel supplied by Shell Germany. During qualifying both cars were fitted with larger turbochargers. Rosberg took pole position on the grid in 1m 32.462s, with Senna second in 1m 32.835s and Prost fourth fastest in 1m 33.335s. Lauda was plagued by a power deficiency in practice and took sixth place on the grid in 1m 33.860s.

Although Rosberg led the race initially, Piquet (Brabham) took the lead on lap 11 and stayed in

front for the remaining 42 laps of the race; these drivers took first and second places. Prost finished third on the same lap as the leaders, ahead of Johansson (Ferrari). Prost *would* have finished second, but Rosberg made a late pit stop for new tyres and snatched second place from Prost on the last lap, by when Prost's rubber was in no state for him to be able to fight back. For much of the race Lauda had led Prost, holding seventh place at the end of lap 1 and coming through to third place by the end of lap 29 when he retired because of transmission problems. It was only too obvious that McLaren had lost the domination which the team had shown in 1984. At this stage in the season Alboreto led the World Championship with 31 points to the 26 of de Angelis and Prost in joint second place.

British Grand Prix

At Silverstone there were no changes to the cars as raced, but during Friday's qualifying the team practised with vertical aerofoils behind the front wheels. Rosberg (Williams) took pole position in 1m 05.591s, with Prost in third place in 1m 06.308s and Lauda back on the fifth row in 1m 07.743s. Initially Senna led from Rosberg, Mansell and Prost. Prost was all set to have a go at passing Mansell, when he slid on oil dropped from Johansson's Ferrari (the result of a first-lap collision with Tambay's Renault) and was lucky to scramble round the corner, dropping back to fifth place behind de Cesaris. By lap 9 Prost was back in third place, and he passed Rosberg on lap 16. By lap 22 Lauda had moved up into third place, but Prost's efforts to catch race leader Senna were unsuccessful. Every time the McLaren closed on the Lotus, the black and gold car pulled away and the Brazilian was able to out-drive the French World Champion until his engine lost its edge. It started to sound very flat, picked up and then on lap 58 went flat again, allowing Prost to sweep through into the lead. Once again the Renault engine of the Lotus picked up and as Prost and Senna lapped Lauda, electrical problems on the second McLaren caused Lauda to baulk his team-mate and Senna was able to pass into the lead as they approached Stowe.

Niki Lauda accelerates away from the pits during qualifying at the 1985 French Grand Prix at the Paul Ricard circuit near Marseille.

The Brazilian led for the whole of the next lap, but again his engine went flat, and whilst Prost sailed by into the lead, Senna crawled round to retire. The Lotus had been eliminated by an electronic fault that had caused the right bank of the Renault V6 to run rich, as a result of which it had run out of fuel. Lauda retired because of electrical problems and so Prost led across the line from Alboreto (Ferrari), a lap in arrears, and Laffite (Ligier). For some incomprehensible reason the race was stopped one lap short, at the end of lap 65, but Prost as a precaution carried on for another lap before pulling into the pits.

In the 1985 French race Nelson Piquet (Brabham BT54) scored his only win of the year, leading across the line Rosberg, seen here following the Brabham, (Williams) and Prost.

German Grand Prix

The McLarens appeared at the Nürburgring, with mirror turbo chargers, that is paired left and right, which permitted the team to improve the airflow to the right turbocharger. In addition the cars now featured new brake calipers with thin metal plates which were intended to aid the circulation of air across the discs and both cars were raced with vertical front aerofoils. As usual the McLarens were not the fastest cars in practice but, surprisingly, pole position went to Teo Fabi with the Toleman-Hart in 1m 17.429s. Prost was third fastest in 1m 18.725s and Lauda was well back on the grid in 12th place in 1m 19.652s. The German Grand Prix was to prove a race of attrition, with race leaders Rosberg and Senna both retiring; Prost was unable to challenge because his car was down on power and after spinning because of fading brakes, he finished second behind Alboreto (Ferrari). Third place went to Laffite with his Ligier and Lauda took fifth place, slowed by the loosening of a rear wheel caused by the incorrect mounting of one of the new brake calipers. Alboreto now led the World Championship with 46 points to the 41 of Prost.

Austrian Grand Prix

At the Austrian race Niki Lauda announced that he proposed retiring from racing at the end of the year. Prost was fastest in practice in 1m 25.490s, for the Österreichring was one of the few circuits on which the TAG engines, which could not be readily boosted for qualifying purposes, could shine in practice through the sweeping bends. Lauda was third fastest in 1m 26.250s. Lauda led away from Prost at

Alain Prost's win in the 1985 British Grand Prix put him back into contention for the World Championship, with 35 points to the 37 of Alboreto.

the start, but because of a multi-car collision further down the grid, the officials decided to stop the race. As the race was now to be run at the full distance again, Prost took the decision to switch to his spare car, because following a jammed throttle in the morning's untimed practice, he had mounted a kerb and hit a bank. The damage had been repaired in good time for the race, but, although just before the start it had been noticed that the right rear universal joint had more play in than was usual, Prost had decided to start the race with this rather than switch to the spare at such a late stage.

At the second start, Prost was away well, ahead of Rosberg and Lauda. Rosberg was an early retirement because of falling oil pressure and Lauda moved up into second place behind Prost, with the two McLarens steadily pulling away from Piquet's Brabham. At the end of lap 26, Prost made a stop for new tyres, rejoining the race in second place behind Lauda, Piquet retired because of a broken exhaust and now Senna held third place behind the two McLarens. On lap 40 the turbocharger broke on Lauda's car and at the end of this 52-lap race Prost led Senna, whose car had been vibrating badly for many laps , by a little over 30 seconds, with the Ferraris of Alboreto and Johansson third and fourth. Alboreto and Prost were now joint leaders in the World Championship with 50 points. In the Constructors' Cup, Ferrari now led by a substantial margin, with 72 points to the 55 of McLaren.

Dutch Grand Prix

At Zandvoort, Piquet was fastest in practice in 1m 11.074s, with Prost third fastest in 1m 11.801s and Lauda back on the fifth row with a time of 1m 13.059s. All these times were set on the Friday, when conditions were warm and dry, as Saturday proved wet. On the Friday Lauda had found that his car was down in power and when it was stripped it was discovered that it had lost compression on one cylinder.

Rosberg led the race initially, but then retired with engine problems and as Prost moved up into the lead, Lauda made an early pit stop for new tyres. By lap 32 the McLarens were first and second, and on lap 33, Prost made his stop for tyres. The McLaren mechanics were not at their quickest and he rejoined the race in third place behind Lauda and Senna. Prost passed Senna for second place on lap 47 and then rapidly closed up on his team-mate. All season Lauda had been turning in lack-lustre performances, just the sort of performances expected from a driver who could not see much of a future ahead of him in racing, but at Zandvoort he fought furiously to keep his team-mate at bay and the two McLaren drivers finished with less than a quarter of a second covering them. Senna took third place, with Alboreto fourth and de Angelis fifth. Alain Prost now led the World Championship, three points clear of Alboreto and McLaren had closed within five points of Ferrari's total in the Constructors' Cup.

Italian Grand Prix

Once again practice was dominated by Senna who took pole position in 1m 25.084s, with Prost fifth fastest in 1m 25.790s and Lauda, plagued by minor problems, back in 16th place on the grid in 1m 28.472s. Initially the race was led by the Williams FW10s of Rosberg and Mansell, with Prost third, moving up to second when Mansell was slowed by a misfiring engine. Prost took the lead when Rosberg stopped for new tyres at the end of lap 28, but by lap 40 Rosberg was in front again. When Rosberg stopped at the pits because of head gasket failure, Prost was unassailable, with a lead of a minute over Piquet (Brabham) and with Senna in third place. Lauda was in ninth place when his engine began to lay a trail of blue smoke. Prost now led the World Championship with 65 points, a comfortable margin of 12 points over Alboreto, whilst in the Constructors' Cup McLaren now had a tenuous lead of 79 points to Ferrari's 77.

In the 1985 Italian Grand Prix at Monza, Lauda retired after leaving a trail of blue smoke.

Belgian Grand Prix

The postponed Belgian Grand Prix was squeezed into the calendar a week after the Monza race and a fortnight before the European Grand Prix at Brands Hatch (a race that itself had been admitted to the calendar to replace the proposed but cancelled New York Grand Prix). Prost took pole position at Spa in 1m 55.306s, with Senna second fastest, despite a spate of blown engines, in 1m 55.403s.

Spa was dominated by the ever-faster, always impressive Ayrton Senna who led throughout with his Lotus 97T-Renault.

Alain Prost in qualifying for the postponed 1985 Belgian Grand Prix in which he drove a steady race to gain Championship points and finished third.

On the Friday during unofficial practice Lauda had been returning to the pits when the throttle jammed open and the car hit the barriers, spraining his right wrist and the Austrian had no alternative but to withdraw from the race. At Spa Senna led throughout to score a fine victory from Mansell (Williams). Prost had held second place initially, on a track that had started wet but gradually dried out and running on unscrubbed slicks, he drove a cautious race for World Championship points rather than outright victory. He eventually took third place to consolidate his Championship lead.

European Grand Prix

By this late stage in the season, it was only too obvious that the immense threat of Ferrari power that had loomed so large earlier in the season, had badly waned and that Prost was now almost unbeatable in the World Championship. For the remaining races of the season McLaren concentrated on steady finishes rather than wins and this policy revealed itself both in practice times and in race results. At the Brands Hatch race former McLaren driver John Watson was brought into the team to partner Prost, as Lauda was still not fit to drive. Senna took pole position in 1m 07.169s, with Prost back in sixth place on the grid in 1m 09.429s. Prost's chief rival in the World Championship, Michele Alboreto, trailing by 19 points, took 15th place on the grid in 1m 10.659s, a tacit admission that Ferrari, plagued by traction problems and engine failures, was conceding any hopes of winning the World Championship. As for Watson, almost two years absence from the wheel of a Formula 1 car showed only too plainly, he had great difficulty in adapting himself to the use of qualifier tyres and to the power and handling of the TAG-powered McLaren and he was back on the 11th row of the grid in 1m 12.496s, ahead only of Jones (Beatrice), Alliot (RAM), Capelli (Tyrrell), Danner (Zakspeed) and Martini (Minardi).

The race was won by Nigel Mansell (Williams) from Ayrton Senna (Lotus) with the second Williams of Rosberg in third place. At the green light Rosberg had made a slow start, causing Prost to pull to the left, putting two wheels on the grass and he was in 14th place at the end of the first lap. He steadily began to work his way through the field; by lap 9 he

John Watson made a comeback to Grand Prix racing at the 1985 European Grand Prix at Brands Hatch, but had difficulty in settling back and finished a poor seventh, two laps in arrears.

had reached sixth place, but he was unhappy with his choice of tyres and although he was due to stop for new tyres of the same type to be fitted at half-distance, he was forced to leave his tyre change to a new mix until lap 38 by when the pit staff were well aware of his needs. At the end of this 75-lap race Prost crossed the line in fourth place, having secured the World Championship for the first time. As for Watson, whilst his confidence and performance improved as the race progressed, he was unable to finish in the points and had to settle for seventh place, two laps in arrears, only too well aware that any Formula 1 comeback was now highly improbable.

1985 World Champion Alain Prost in that year's South African Grand Prix. He finished third behind the Williams FW10s of Nigel Mansell and Keke Rosberg.

South African Grand Prix

At this race Prost appeared with a new McLaren chassis, MP4/2B-6, the first carbon-fibre monocoque to be built entirely at the McLaren works at Woking. Lauda was back in the team at Kyalami, but neither driver was happy with his car during qualifying. Although the McLarens were fitted with modified turbochargers and turbo compressors, the high altitude at Kyalami caused problems. Lauda took eighth place on the grid in 1m 04.283s with Prost one place slower in 1m 04.376s, the only time in two seasons that Lauda had qualified faster than Prost. Nigel Mansell took pole position in 1m 02.366s with his Williams FW10 and led throughout the race to take a well deserved victory.

Nigel Mansell, winner of the 1985 South African Grand Prix with the Honda-powered Williams FW10.

Alain Prost in the pits at the 1985 Australian Grand Prix. He retired because of engine problems.

For much of the race Alain Prost held second place, with Lauda third. Lauda took second place briefly for two laps, laps 35 and 36, whilst Prost was in the pits for new tyres, but just as he was about to take the lead from Mansell, he retired with a blown turbocharger. Prost finished third behind the two Williams entries of Mansell and Rosberg.

Australian Grand Prix

On the difficult Adelaide street circuit, the McLarens were again in trouble, for Prost's car was handling badly and Lauda was unhappy with the number of laps, some five or six, needed to warm up his tyres. Senna took pole position in 1m 19.843s, his seventh pole position of the season, followed by Mansell and Rosberg, with Prost, despite his problems, in fourth place in 1m 21.889s. Lauda was well back on the grid in 1m 23.941s. Initially Rosberg led from Senna, with Alboreto third and Prost fourth. Prost moved into third place when Alboreto made an early stop for new tyres, was briefly passed by Surer but the McLaren driver soon went ahead again only to retire on lap 27 with a major engine failure. The order was now Rosberg, Senna, Surer, and with Lauda in fourth place. When Rosberg slowed to pull into the pits for new tyres, he was clipped by Senna's Lotus.

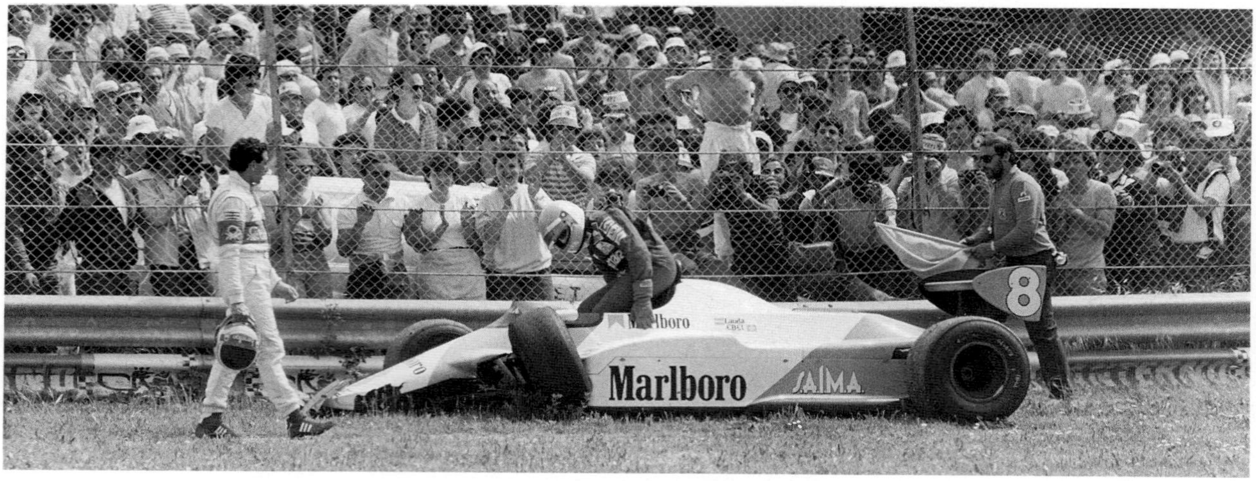

In his last race, the 1985 Australian Grand Prix, Niki Lauda crashed his McLaren into a retaining wall because of brake problems. Here, as he climbs out of his MP4/2B, Patrese, who had retired his Benetton earlier, walks over to commiserate.

The Lotus lost its right front aerofoil against the left rear wing side-plate of the Williams, and on the next lap Senna slid violently across the kerbing on to the outside of the circuit, motoring across the grass to rejoin the track on the other side of the hairpin and finally stopping for new tyres and a new nose section at the end of the following lap. Surer retired with engine failure and so the order was Rosberg, Lauda and Senna. When Rosberg stopped for his third tyre change and Senna's brakes faded, Lauda took the lead briefly on lap 56, but he too had been having trouble with his brakes and at the right-hand corner at the end of the main straight the rear brakes locked and the McLaren bent its left front suspension against the retaining wall. Senna retired with engine trouble and Rosberg won the race from the Ligiers of Laffite and Streiff.

Consistency and a constant well managed development programme were McLaren's strongest cards in 1985. The early promise showed by Ferrari faded, and whilst both Lotus and Williams displayed supremacy during parts of the year, both lacked the consistency of development to maintain themselves at the forefront. At the final count Prost's lead in the World Championship was by 20 points over Alboreto, and McLaren won the Constructors' Cup with 90 points against the 82 of Ferrari, and the 71 each of Williams and Lotus.

5: 1986: The Closest Year

For 1986 John Barnard produced the improved MP4/2C, of which three new chassis were ready at the start of the season. There were no substantial changes from the 1985 cars, despite the fact that there was now a fuel capacity restriction of 195 litres. The driver was seated in a lower, more reclined position and there were internal panels added to the monocoque to accommodate the smaller fuel cell. A 6-speed gearbox was now standard and there were other changes to the transmission of a minor nature. McLaren had been working with SEP on a carbon-fibre clutch which had first been tried in 1985 and although it was used throughout 1986 as part of the team's development programme, it was not raced. Following Niki Lauda's retirement from racing Alain Prost was joined in the team by former Williams driver Keke Rosberg, who was himself to retire at the end of the year.

Other teams had made more dramatic changes for the new year, including Ferrari who had introduced the completely new F1/86 car, Brabham who had produced the revolutionary BT55 with BMW turbocharged engine laid on its side and a 7-speed gearbox, whilst the Benetton team, an ever growing power in motor racing, had taken over the Toleman team and was running the B186 (formerly TG186) cars with turbocharged BMW engines. Lotus had produced the 98T, generally a refined and improved version of the 1985 97T, whilst Williams had produced the FW11 which the team called 'a logical development of the 1985 car', but was totally new although without dramatic changes. It was the Williams team with Mansell and Piquet as drivers, together with Senna (Lotus) that were to prove the most serious threats to McLaren's supremacy in 1986. Having one top-line driver, Senna, backed up by a newcomer who was not capable of contending for the lead (Johnny Dumfries) and the fact that the 98T was generally less reliable than the Williams and McLaren opposition resulted in the comparative lack of success of the Lotus team.

Brazilian Grand Prix

Maintaining the supremacy in speed that he had displayed in 1985 Senna took pole position at Rio de Janeiro in 1m 25.501s, with Piquet and Mansell in second and third places on the grid. Prost, after troubled qualifying sessions, was ninth on the grid in 1m 28.099s, two places behind his new team-mate Rosberg who recorded 1m 27.705s. Prost gradually worked his way through from 11th place at the end of lap 1 to take the lead from Senna on lap 20, just before Senna pulled into the pits for new tyres. Eight laps later Prost stopped for tyres himself, rejoined the race in third place, but only two laps later he was out with piston failure, the result of a problem with the electronic box causing incorrect fuel mixture to reach the cylinder, a problem that had already eliminated Rosberg. Right at the start of the race Senna had tangled with Mansell who had hit the barrier, and he eventually finished second behind Piquet, with the Ligiers of Laffite and Arnoux in third and fourth places.

Spanish Grand Prix

Five years had elapsed since the last Spanish race, held at Jarama, and on its revival the race was run on a well equipped, but bumpy and boring new circuit at Jerez in Spain's sherry country. Once again practice was dominated by Ayrton Senna, whose spare 98T was set up in full qualifying trim, with stiff suspension and in the words of Senna 'bottoming out everywhere'. His pole position time was 1m 21.605s, around 30 seconds faster than experts had expected to be achieved at the circuit. Once again the Williams FW11s occupied second and third places on the grid, with Prost fourth fastest in 1m 22.886s and Rosberg fifth with a time of 1m 23.004s. Rosberg in particular was pleased with his practice time and confided that he felt that he was now getting the hang of the McLaren. As he had dominated practice, so Senna dominated much of the race, but on lap 40 he was passed by second-place man Mansell who squeezed Senna against Brundle (Tyrrell) as he and the Brazilian lapped the slower British driver. Soon Mansell had pulled out a lead of 3.5 seconds, but then Mansell began to slow because a rear tyre had picked up debris and was losing pressure. Prost was now in third place and both he and Senna were worrying at Mansell's exhausts. Senna pulled into the lead on lap 68 whilst Mansell headed for the pits and a tyre change, and rejoined the race in third place. He forced his way past the McLaren and rapidly made up ground on the leading Lotus. At the end of the 72-lap race Senna crossed the line with Mansell almost alongside, to produce the closest Grand Prix finish since the 1971 Italian race. Prost and Rosberg took third and fourth places. At this stage in the season Senna led the World Championship with 15 points to the 9 of Piquet and 6 of Mansell, with Prost fourth equal with 4 points.

San Marino Grand Prix

At Imola Senna again took pole position, ahead of Piquet and Williams with Prost fourth on the grid. Senna's pole was in 1m 25.050s, whilst Prost recorded 1m 26.176s and Rosberg was two places

Alain Prost in the 1986 Spanish Grand Prix at the new Jerez circuit where he finished third behind Senna (Lotus) and Mansell (Williams).

In the 1986 San Marino Grand Prix at Imola Keke Rosberg took fifth place after running out of fuel. The race was won by Alain Prost.

slower in 1m 26.385s. Although rain threatened, the race was run in dry conditions. Piquet took the lead on the first lap from Senna, with Prost third and Rosberg fourth. Rosberg passed Prost to hold second place, but the leading positions changed again during routine tyre stops. Piquet's stop was longer than expected, Prost made a very good stop and once they were all back on the road Prost led from Rosberg and Piquet. Two laps from the finish Rosberg's McLaren ran out of fuel despite the fact that the on-board computer indicated that there was plenty left. On the very last lap Prost too ran out of fuel, but by weaving the McLaren he managed to get the engine to pick up enough fuel to boost the car towards the finish and allow him to coast to the line. Piquet took second place ahead of Berger (Benetton), Johansson and Rosberg. It was only too obvious that on some circuits the new 195 litres fuel capacity limit was to prove critical.

Monaco Grand Prix

Despite clipping a barrier on the Thursday, Prost took pole position in 1m 22.627s, with Mansell second in 1m 23.047s. Senna not displaying his usual speed was third fastest in 1m 23.175s. Rosberg

In this shot of the early laps of the San Marino Grand Prix Rosberg leads Prost.

was back on the fifth row with a time of 1m 24.701s. Prost led the 78-lap race throughout, except after his pit stop for new tyres when Senna took the lead and when Senna made his pit stop, Rosberg moved up into second place. These were the finishing positions, with Senna third and Mansell fourth, ahead of the Ligiers of Arnoux and Laffite. Prost was now third in the World Championship with 13 points to the 15 of joint leaders Senna and Piquet, whilst McLaren had 18 points in the Constructors' Cup to the 21 points of Williams.

Belgian Grand Prix

Almost remarkably, at Spa-Francorchamps, Senna was pushed off the front row of the grid by Piquet who took pole position in 1m 54.331s and with Berger (Benetton) alongside him in 1m 54.468s and Prost third fastest in 1m 54.501s. Rosberg was eighth fastest in 1m 55.662s. It was not to be a McLaren race. At the start Senna accelerated through from the second row moving over to run round the left side of Berger and as Senna, Berger and Prost lined up into La Source, the McLaren and Benetton locked wheels and both cars turned to the left. Prost's airborne McLaren crashed on to the kerbing on the outside of the corner, blocking the field, but both he and Berger were able to carry on to make pit stops at the end of the first lap. After the nose-cone had been replaced on Prost's McLaren he drove a steady, but solitary race through the field to finish sixth. Rosberg avoided the mêlée, but retired on lap 7 with engine problems. The race was won by Mansell from Senna and the Ferraris of Johansson and Alboreto.

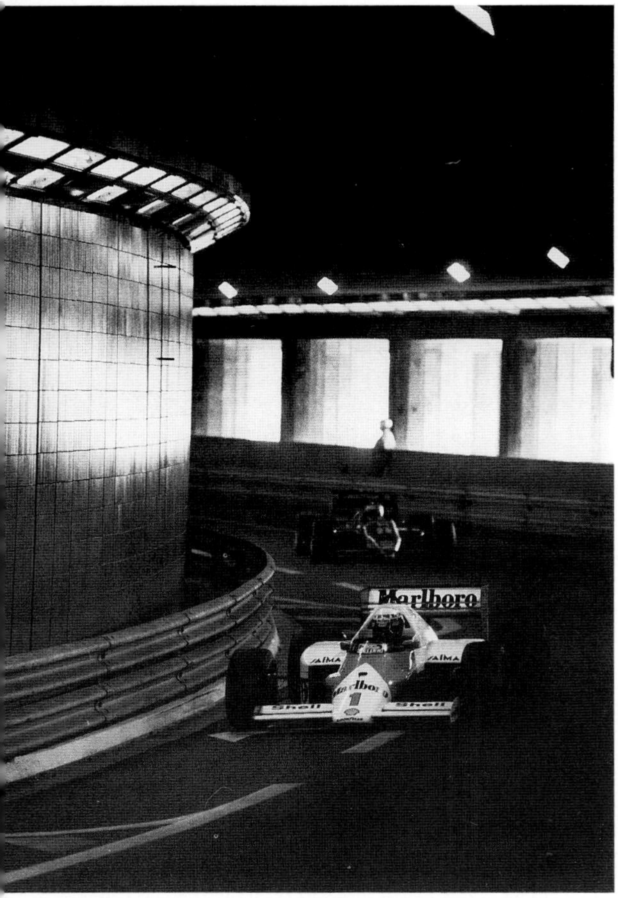

Alain Prost passes through the tunnel on his way to victory in the 1986 Monaco Grand Prix.

Canadian Grand Prix

Because, historically, the Canadian race was one that proved marginal on fuel for most teams, Bosch had carried out revisions to the Motronic fuel management system of the TAG engines. There was now a fuel pump modified to run separate feeds to each bank of cylinders. Mansell was fastest in practice in 1m 24.118s, with Senna second in 1m 24.188s. Prost was fourth fastest with a time of 1m 25.192s and Rosberg sixth fastest in 1m 25.33s. Qualifying was not troublefree, for Prost was complaining that the revs were dropping so low at the hairpin bends that the engine was almost dying. Qualifying on the Friday was cool and damp, but on the hot sunny afternoon of Saturday both McLarens were understeering badly and this particularly upset Rosberg. At the start Mansell led away from Senna and Prost, with Rosberg fifth. At the pits hairpin on lap 4 Rosberg locked a front wheel and was close to colliding with the gearbox of Prost. Prost took second place from Senna, with the Brazilian fighting all the way, sliding badly and allowing Rosberg to slip through on the straight that followed. When Prost made his routine stop for new tyres at the end of lap 31, there was a delay in the pits because a front wheel nut jammed and he rejoined the race in fifth place. After Senna and Piquet made their stops, the order was Mansell, Rosberg and Prost. Piquet fought his way back through to second place, but was forced to stop to change blistered rear tyres shortly before the finish so the order at the chequered flag was Mansell – Prost – Piquet – Rosberg who had been forced to ease back to conserve fuel after his hectic pace in the opening laps. This was Mansell's second consecutive Grand Prix win and it was beginning to look as though he was the driver for the other teams to beat.

Keke Rosberg pulled off early in the 1986 Belgian Grand Prix because of engine trouble.

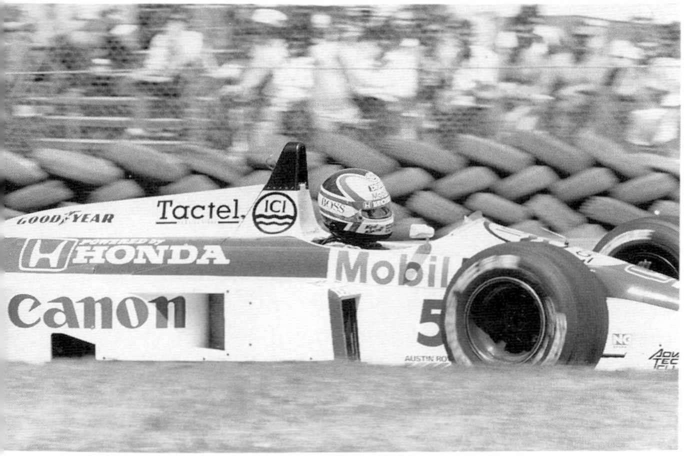

Nigel Mansell, winner of the 1986 Canadian Grand Prix at the wheel of his Honda-powered Williams FW11.

United States Grand Prix (Detroit)

At the Detroit street circuit, the McLarens were unchanged, but qualifying was again far from trouble-free, for Prost crashed into the wall at the exit from the chicane. Pole position went to Senna in 1m 38.301s, whilst Prost was back on the fourth row in 1m 40.715s, with Rosberg two places further back in 1m 40.848s. Both McLarens had been plagued by lack of traction and on the Friday they had run extra fuel to try to prevent the rear wheels from spinning. The race proved very much of a battle between Senna and the two Williams FW11s of Mansell and Piquet, but Piquet crashed and Mansell dropped back to finish fifth. Senna won the race, whilst Prost, whose TAG engine was suffering from one of its occasional bouts of cutting in and cutting out, was unable to challenge for the lead, was passed by Laffite's Ligier and the World Champion was obliged to settle for third place. Rosberg retired early in the race because of transmission problems. Senna now led the World Championship with 36 points to the 33 of Prost and with Mansell in third place with 29 points.

French Grand Prix

At the Paul Ricard circuit Senna again took pole in 1m 06.526s, with Mansell second fastest in 1m 06.755s. As usual, handicapped by lack of bhp in qualifying, Prost was back in fifth place in 1m 07.266s, complaining of poor throttle response,

In the 1986 French Grand Prix at the Paul Ricard circuit Keke Rosberg, who finished fourth, leads Johnny Dumfries (Lotus 98T).

and Rosberg was two places lower on the grid in 1m 07.545s. At the start Mansell took the lead from Senna with Arnoux (Ligier) third, Berger (Benetton) fourth and Prost fifth. On lap 4 Senna slid into a tyre barrier, tearing a front wheel off the Lotus, Berger was put out of contention by a collision with Danner's Arrows and soon Prost and Rosberg had moved ahead of Mansell. At this race the Williams team had taken a calculated gamble, reckoning that lap time saved by new rubber would compensate for the time wasted in the pits and the FW11s of both Mansell and Piquet made two pit stops for new tyres. Prost led again whilst Mansell made his second tyre stop, but at the finish the British driver was over 26 seconds ahead of Prost with Piquet third and Rosberg fourth. Now Mansell was only one point behind Prost in the World Championship (38 points to 39) and Senna was third with 36 points.

British Grand Prix

At Brands Hatch McLaren used heated tyres for the first time during qualifying. Prost also tried during qualifying a different front suspension geometry. Practice was dominated by the FW11s with Piquet taking pole position in 1m 06.961s and Mansell second on the grid in 1m 07.399s. On this circuit Rosberg was faster than his team-mate, fifth fastest in 1m 08.477s, with Prost next on the grid in 1m 09.334s. A collision at Paddock Hill bend caused the race to be stopped and re-started. The British Grand Prix was dominated by the Williams FW11s of Mansell and Piquet, although Berger (Benetton) made a charge in the opening laps holding second place for two laps before dropping back to third place until eliminated by electrical problems. Mansell and Piquet took the first two places, with Prost third, Arnoux (Ligier) fourth and the Tyrrells of Brundle and Streiff fifth and sixth. Rosberg was the first retirement in the race with gearbox problems.

German Grand Prix

During the week before the German Grand Prix Ron Dennis and Alain Prost had visited Honda in Japan to try and tie up a deal for the use of Honda V6 engines in 1987. However, it seemed that the approach was premature, for Honda had agreed to supply engines to Team Lotus for 1987 and it had also been agreed that the Williams team would remain a Honda user during the coming year.

At Hockenheim the McLarens appeared with new KKK turbochargers and with revised fuel injection systems which had been previously tested at Silverstone and a clear improvement in power during qualifying was obvious. Rosberg took pole position on the grid in 1m 42.013s, with Prost second fastest in 1m 42.166s and Senna third in 1m 42.329s. Constantly banging at the door was Berger with the Benetton, fourth fastest in 1m 42.541s.

In the German race Prost ran out of fuel and was classified sixth, a lap in arrears.

McLaren International's stock of spare TAG engines at the 1986 German Grand Prix.

When the light turned green, Rosberg made a slow start, Senna accelerated into the lead clouting Prost's right front wheel and so Senna led away from Berger, Rosberg, Piquet and Prost. Rosberg took the lead on lap 2, Berger stopped at the pits because of a leaking intercooler and Piquet went ahead of Rosberg. Prost held third place with Senna fourth. Piquet made an unscheduled stop for tyres and Mansell's Williams was handling far from well. So Prost and Rosberg settled into 1-2 at the head of the field leading Senna. After Piquet's second stop for tyres, he resumed in third place, but the Williams had the legs of the McLarens and took the lead again. Both McLarens ran out of fuel and were classified fifth (Rosberg) and sixth (Prost) behind Piquet, Senna, Mansell and Arnoux. With a lucky third place, Mansell extended his lead in the World Championship to 51 points, with Prost second with 44 points and Senna third with 42.

Hungarian Grand Prix

The race on the new Hungaroring was the first World Championship event ever to be held in a Warsaw Pact country. The new circuit was well laid out and organization was superb, but there were rather too many slow and boring corners. Because of the new surface, most drivers used soft race tyres during Friday's qualifying, reserving the slicks for the Saturday when there was a good coating of rubber and oil on the circuit. Senna took pole position in 1m 29.450s, with Piquet second fastest, Prost third (1m 29.945s), Mansell fourth and Rosberg fifth (1m 30.638s). During Saturday's qualifying Prost had tried out titanium vertical fins fitted to the underside of the rear diffuser and these were adopted on both cars on race day. Because his engine died on the warm-up lap, Prost was forced to switch to the spare McLaren at the last moment.

In Hungary the McLarens were never in contention for the lead. Early in the race Prost made a pit stop for new tyres, and he lost eight laps whilst an electronic problem was resolved. Whilst Prost's McLaren was stationary in the pits, Rosberg came in for new tyres, but was quickly waved away and accelerated hard back into the race. Although other teams were using radio communication with the cars, this had not yet been adopted by McLaren. Rosberg returned to the pits a lap later because a rear tyre was losing air, he climbed back to sixth place, stopped again because of a deflating tyre and retired because the rear suspension had been damaged. Prost in the meanwhile had been eliminated in a collision with Arnoux. Piquet won the race from Senna and Mansell.

Alain Prost in the 1986 Hungarian Grand Prix on the new Hungaroring circuit in which he was eliminated by a crash with René Arnoux (Ligier).

Austrian Grand Prix

Qualifying at the Österreichring revealed the growing power of the Benetton team and Fabi (1m 23.549s) and Berger (1m 23.743s) took first two places on the grid ahead of Rosberg (1m 23.903s), with Prost fifth fastest in 1m 24.346s. From the start the Benettons led the race, but Fabi retired because of engine failure on lap 17 and Berger developed a bad engine misfire on the lap prior to a routine pit stop for tyres. The problem was a broken battery and he lost five laps before rejoining the race. Mansell then took the lead, but when he was eliminated by a drive-shaft constant velocity joint failure, Prost moved up into first place with Rosberg second. On lap 48 of this 52-lap race Rosberg stopped because of electrical problems and Prost went on to score his third race win of the season ahead of the Ferraris of Alboreto and Johansson.

Italian Grand Prix

At Monza the Benettons were again to the fore, with Fabi taking pole position in 1m 24.078s, and Berger fourth fastest in 1m 24.885s. Prost was second fastest in 1m 24.514s with Rosberg back in eighth position in 1m 25.378s. Before the parade lap Prost's McLaren refused to fire because of a faulty alternator and was forced to run to the spare car. Fabi's Benetton also refused to fire initially and joined the back of the grid, whilst in accordance with race regulations Prost started from the pit lane. As a result, Mansell and Berger headed the grid, Berger led for the first four laps and then the race settled down to a dominant Williams pattern with Mansell heading Piquet. Berger led briefly whilst Mansell was in the pits for new tyres, but the finishing order was Piquet – Mansell – Johansson – Rosberg.

For Alain Prost it proved a thoroughly miserable race. After starting from the pit lane behind the rest of the field, he fought his way back to hold sixth place by lap 18 behind team-mate Rosberg. The stewards had, however, decided that Prost should be disqualified for breaking the rule that permitted no

Keke Rosberg with his MP4/2C in the pits at the 1986 Austrian Grand Prix.

At the Österreichring Alain Prost scored one of his few wins of 1986, leading across the line the Ferraris of Alboreto and Johansson.

Left: Alain Prost at the wheel of his McLaren MP4/2B at the 1985 Brazilian Grand Prix, the first of the season's races.

1985

Below: In the Brazilian race Prost scored yet another fine victory ahead of Alboreto's Ferrari and set fastest lap.

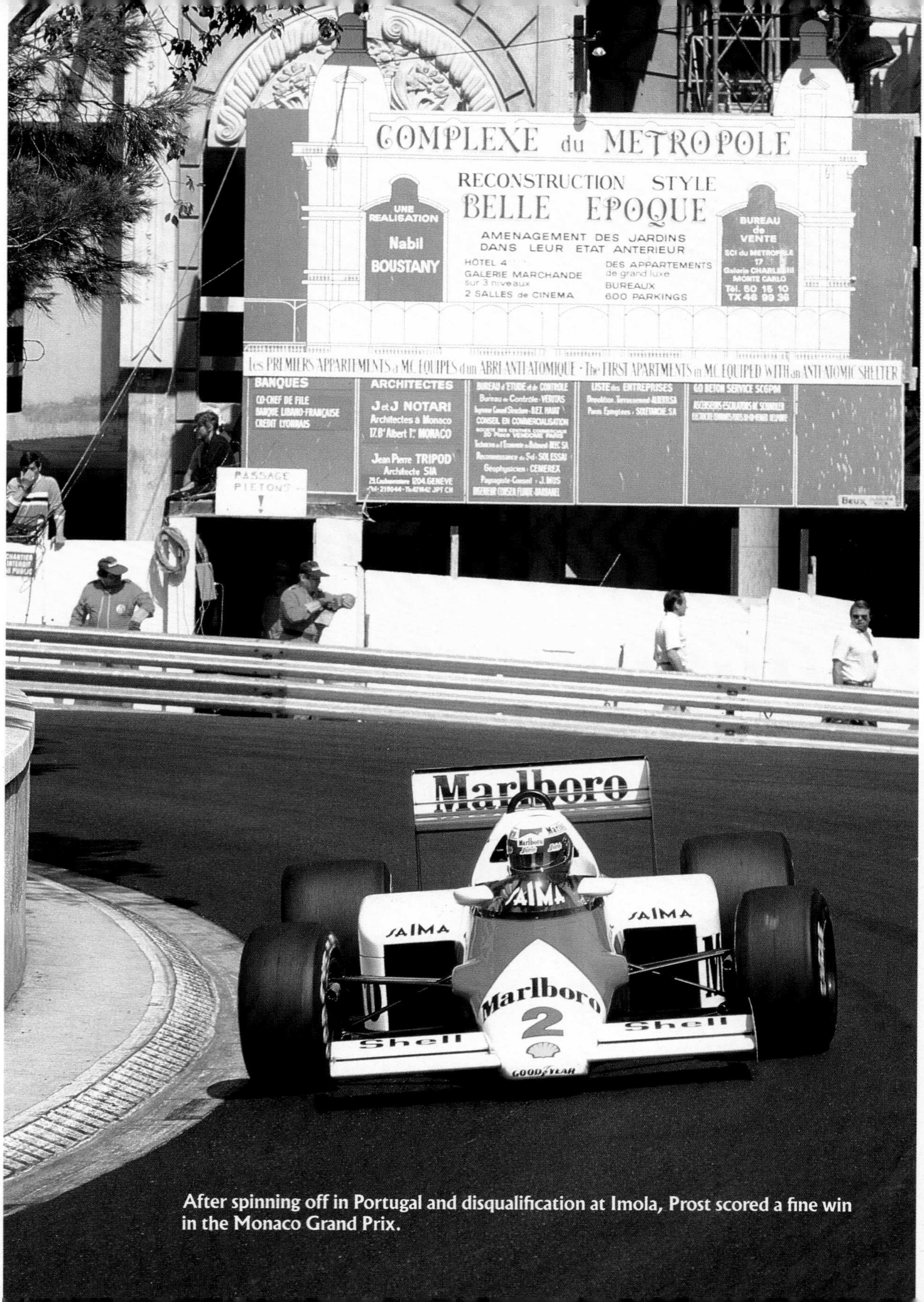

After spinning off in Portugal and disqualification at Imola, Prost scored a fine win in the Monaco Grand Prix.

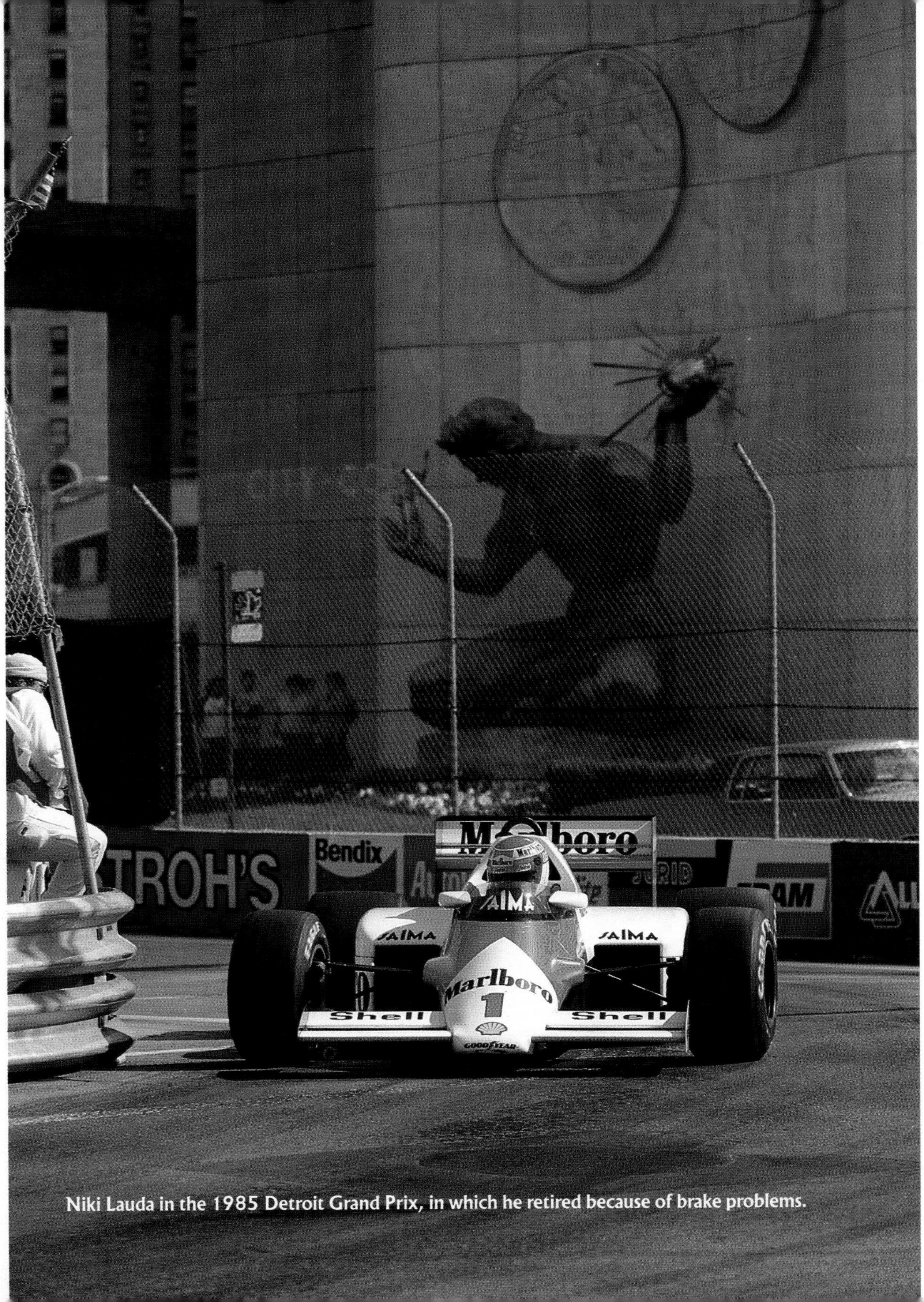

Niki Lauda in the 1985 Detroit Grand Prix, in which he retired because of brake problems.

Above: Niki Lauda during pre-race testing at Silverstone before the 1985 British Grand Prix.

Right: After Prost's victory in the British Grand Prix, his MP4/2B is weighed at post-race scrutineering.

Keeping a check on the opposition, Ron Dennis (left) and Alain Prost watch practice times during qualifying at the 1985 Austrian Grand Prix.

Alain Prost won the Austrian Grand Prix from Ayrton Senna's Lotus and was now equal first in the Championship with Michele Alboreto (Ferrari).

Alain Prost in the wet at the Belgian Grand Prix at Spa-Francorchamps. He finished third behind Senna (Lotus) and Mansell (Williams).

John Watson, making a return to Formula 1 after nearly two years, was brought into the McLaren team at the European Grand Prix at Brands Hatch after Lauda injured his wrist at Spa. Never able to get to grips with the McLaren, Watson finished seventh, two laps in arrears.

Top Left: Keke Rosberg, the 1982 World Champion, who quit the Williams team at the end of 1985 for a final season with McLaren before retiring.

1986

Bottom Left: Rosberg at the wheel of his McLaren MP4/2C at Rio de Janeiro.

Bottom Right: Refreshment for Alain Prost at th
1986 Brazilian Grand Prix.

Keke Rosberg's McLaren MP4/2C at the Brazilian Grand Prix. In this race both McLarens retired because of engine problems.

Alain Prost in the 1986 San Marino Grand Prix which he won from Nelson Piquet (Williams). After this race Prost led the World Championship.

Left: The McLaren mechanics working on one of the MP4/2Cs at Monaco in 1986.

Below: At Monaco Prost took pole position, won after leading for most of the race, and set fastest lap.

Bottom: Keke Rosberg finished second at Monaco, his best performance so far that year.

The magnificent Bedford transporter of the McLaren team.

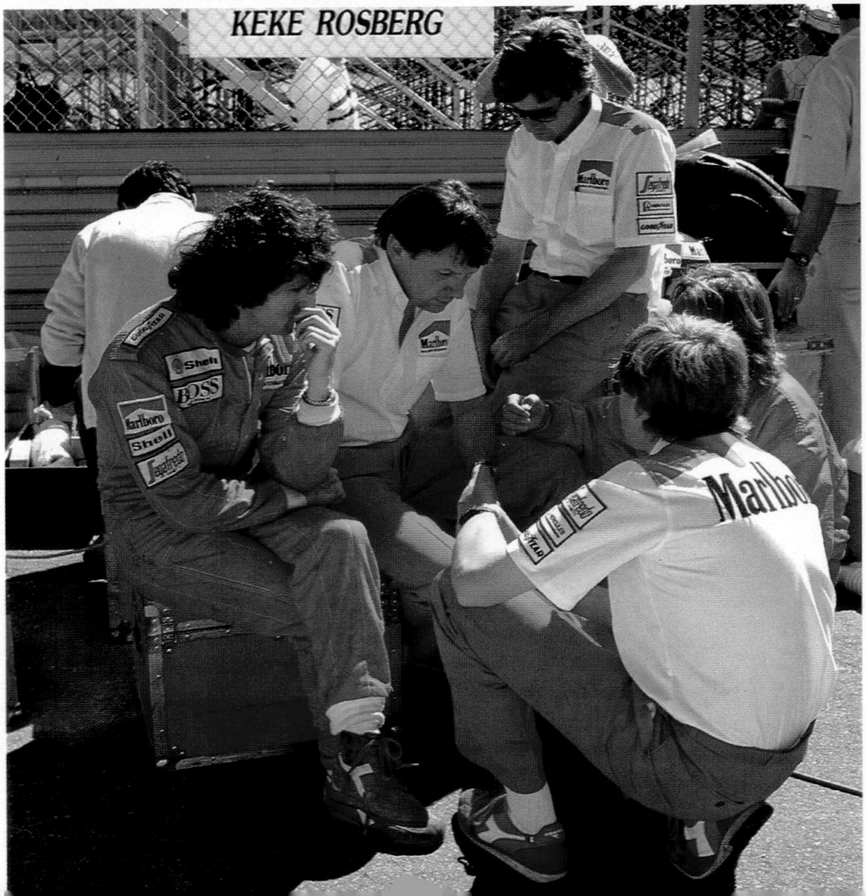

The Williams opposition and Senna (Lotus) were all faster than the McLaren drivers at Montreal in 1986. Here the McLaren team looks almost dejected at their debriefing at the Canadian race.

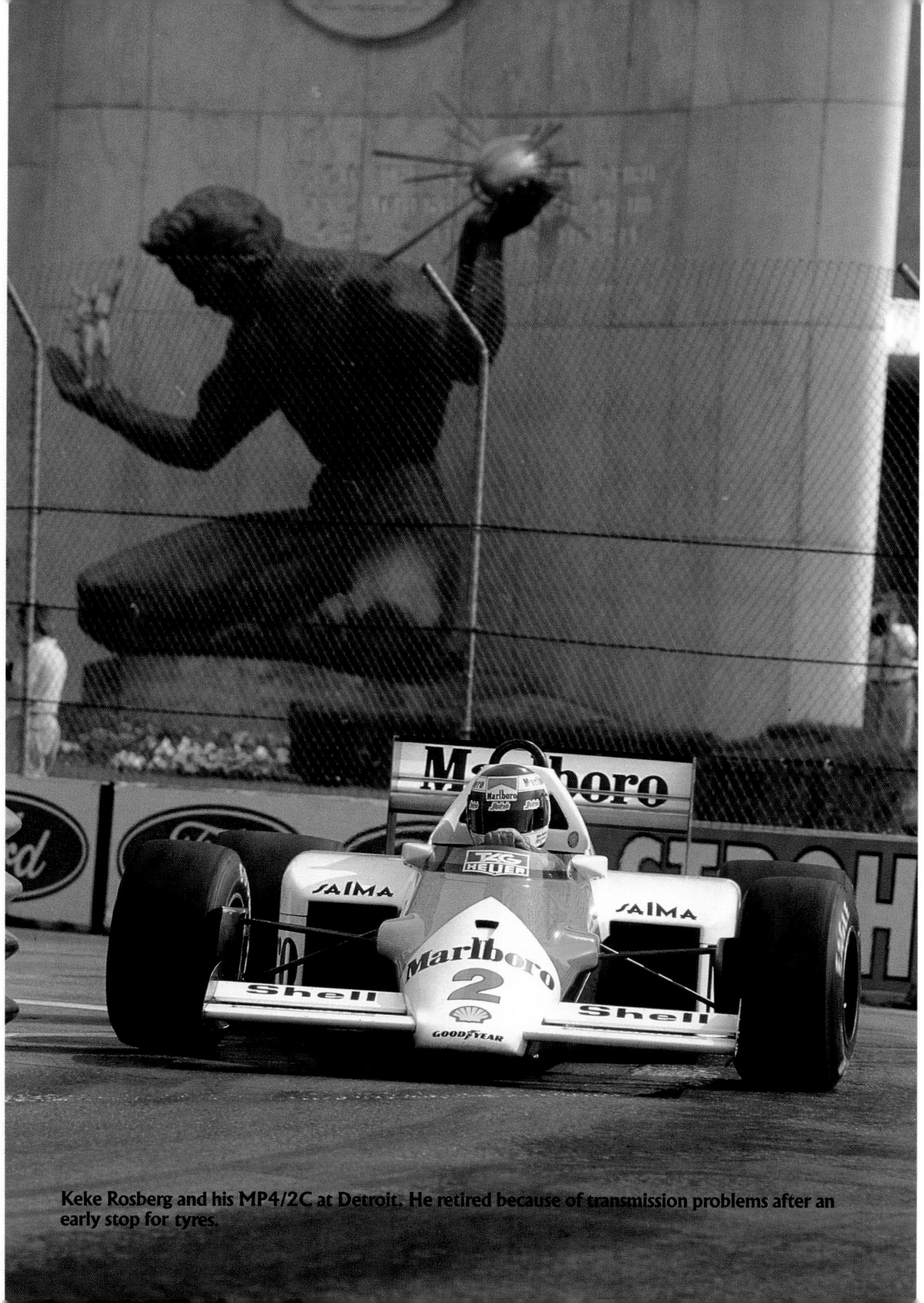

Keke Rosberg and his MP4/2C at Detroit. He retired because of transmission problems after an early stop for tyres.

Right: Alain Prost in the 1986 French Grand Prix at the Paul Ricard circuit. He finished second to Nigel Mansell (Williams-Honda). After this race Prost, with 39 points, led the World Championship by one point from Mansell.

Below: Keke Rosberg in the 1986 British Grand Prix. He retired early in the race because of gearbox failure.

Keke Rosberg in the 1986 Italian Grand Prix. In this race Rosberg finished fourth behind the Williams-Hondas of Piquet and Mansell and Johansson's Ferrari.

change of car after the green flag had been shown for the start of the parade lap. Once McLaren's Director Ron Dennis had been told of the intended disqualification he argued furiously with the stewards and so it was not until the end of lap 26 that the black flag with Prost's number was displayed. Prost did not come into the pits immediately and two laps later the McLaren's engine failed in a cloud of blue smoke. After the race Prost, furious that he had been allowed to race for over half an hour and even to make a pit stop for a new nose-cone to be fitted without being stopped, spoke out freely to the press and as a result was fined by FISA $5000. It was beginning to look as though Prost had lost the World Championship, for Mansell now led with 61 points to the 56 of his team-mate Piquet and his own 53.

Portuguese Grand Prix

At Estoril McLaren appeared with a new car, MP4/2C-4. The most important changes to the McLarens could not be seen, for Porsche had made major engine modifications. Senna took pole position for the seventh time in 1986 with a lap in 1m 16.673s, with Mansell second fastest in 1m 17.489s, Prost third in 1m 17.710s and Berger fourth with a lap in 1m 17.742s. Rosberg was back in seventh place with a lap in 1m 18.360s. The race was to prove a magnificent triumph for Nigel Mansell, for not only did he lead throughout to win at 116.596 mph, but he set fastest lap at 120.216 mph. Prost had run steadily in fourth place for most

The McLaren team practises wheel-changes at the 1986 Portuguese Grand Prix at Estoril.

of the race, displacing Piquet on lap 64 and moving up to second place on the last lap when Senna's Lotus ran low on fuel. Rosberg retired with engine failure on lap 42 when holding fifth place. In the World Championship Mansell now led with 70 points, to the 60 of Piquet and 59 of Prost.

Mexican Grand Prix

Apart from larger compressors on the turbochargers there were only detailed changes to the McLarens at Mexico City. Senna took his eighth pole position of the season in 1m 16.990s, while Prost was back in sixth place with a lap in 1m 18.421s and Rosberg was five places slower in 1m 19.342s. Initially Piquet led from Senna, who had locked his brakes at the first right-hand corner, with Berger third and Prost fourth. When Piquet and Senna stopped for new tyres, Berger assumed what everyone thought would be a short-lived lead, but he had resolved to drive through without a stop for tyres and handling his car with intelligence and conserving fuel he came through to win the race by a margin of just over 25 seconds from Prost, with Senna third and Piquet fourth. Rosberg retired because of a punctured tyre.

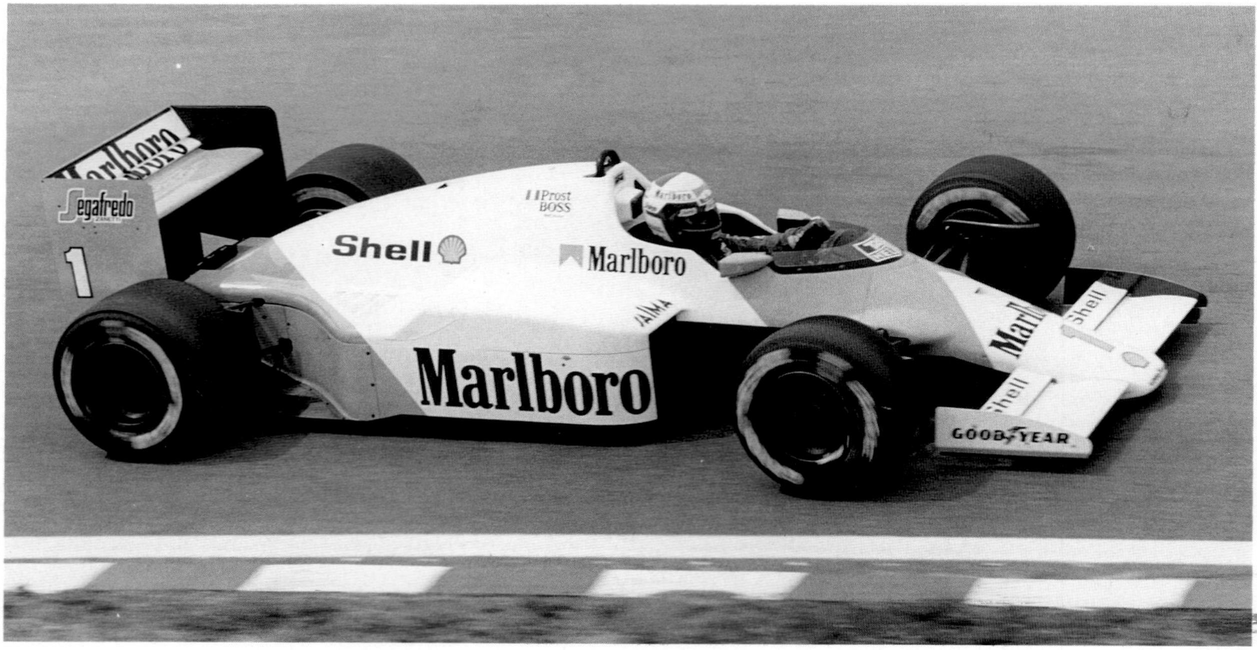

Alain Prost on his way to second place to Nigel Mansell (Williams-Honda) at Estoril.

At Mexico City in 1986 Gerhard Berger scored an unexpected but well-deserved victory with the Benetton-BMW.

The start of the 1986 Australian Grand Prix at Adelaide.

Nigel Mansell (Williams-Honda) who lost the 1986 World Championship because of tyre failure in the Australian race.

Alain Prost won the Australian race and the World Championship by the narrow margin of two points.

Australian Grand Prix

The McLarens were fitted with larger turbochargers at Adelaide, but they were still not able to vie for pole position on the grid. Fastest in qualifying was Mansell in 1m 18.403s, with Piquet second fastest in 1m 18.714s. Prost took fourth place on the grid in 1m 19.654s. Rosberg was seventh fastest in 1m 20.778s. Before the start of this race Mansell led the World Championship with 70 points (72 gross) to the 64 of Prost (65 gross) and so there was a chance of Prost winning the World Championship, provided that he won the race.

Piquet led initially, but then Rosberg went ahead holding first place for lap after lap, whilst Prost fought his way to the front, moving into third place ahead of Mansell on lap 12 and second ahead of Piquet on lap 21. When Prost lapped Berger on lap 32, he hit the Benetton, a tyre deflated and he was forced to stop for a wheel change, rejoining the race in fourth place. Mansell seemed secure in third position, and it looked as though Rosberg was going to win at least one race that year. On lap 63 Rosberg however, heard a rumbling noise from the rear of his McLaren, believing the engine had run its bearings, he switched off and coasted to a halt. Only after he had climbed out of the car did he realise that the right rear tyre had started to delaminate and that strips of rubber were banging against the bodywork.

The whole face of the race and the Championship changed on lap 64 when Mansell's left-rear Goodyear tyre exploded as he was travelling at around 180 mph in sixth gear. Fighting desperately for control, and with the left-rear corner of the Williams throwing up a shower of sparks, Mansell managed to steer the car up the escape road beyond the hairpin bend. Because of this tyre problem, Goodyear advised the Williams pit that Piquet should be called in for a tyre change, which allowed Prost into the lead and at the finish Prost was just over four seconds ahead of Piquet. Prost however, had been quite convinced that he would not make it to the end, because his computer readout showed that he was five litres short of fuel to finish. He had no alternative but to press on and hope the computer readout was faulty – which it proved to be.

For all British enthusiasts Mansell's defeat in the World Championship by a deflating tyre rather than being outdriven by the opposition was a sad blow. Prost won the Championship with 72 points (74 gross) to the 70 of Mansell (72 gross), whilst Williams completely dominated the Constructors' Cup with a grand total of 141 points compared to the 96 of McLaren and 58 of Lotus. It had been a magnificent, hard-fought season and the following year was to see a swing of fortunes in favour of the Williams team.

6: 1987: McLaren Eclipsed

John Barnard had left McLaren International in August 1986 to set up for Ferrari the Guildford Technical Office where he would develop a new breed of Maranello contenders. His place at McLaren was taken by Steve Nichols, promoted from within the team, and subsequently the design staff were joined by Gordon Murray and Neil Oatley. The 1987 MP4/3 represented a progressive, almost conservative development of the 1986 car. The monocoque was lower and slimmer behind the cockpit, there was modified front suspension geometry, underbody and aerodynamics, and the previous combined water/oil radiators had been replaced by vertical radiators, with oil heat exchangers mounted between the water radiators and the intercoolers. During the year five cars were built, three of which were just completed in time for the first race of the season in Brazil. In the knowledge that the team would be using Honda engines in 1988, a sixth chassis was completed to take the Honda V6 unit. Alain Prost remained with McLaren and now that Keke Rosberg had retired, the team was joined by Stephan Johansson, who had been replaced at Ferrari by Gerhard Berger.

Throughout the year the dominant team proved to be Williams with their Honda-powered FW11B cars driven by Nigel Mansell and Nelson Piquet, whilst Ayrton Senna, in his last season with Lotus, also using Honda engines, was to give his all and to take third place in the World Championship. Albeit temporarily, McLarens slipped from their position of supremacy and it seemed, mistakenly, that the great days of the team were perhaps already over.

There were two important changes in racing in 1987. The first was that the introduction of a four-bar turbocharger limit controlled by pop-off valves brought to an end the era of unlimited power of turbocharged engines and now that Goodyear alone were supplying tyres in Formula 1, it had been agreed that there would no longer be available the super-soft super-sticky qualifying tyres.

Brazilian Grand Prix

In practice the Williams team displayed that they had the perfectly developed package and Mansell and Piquet took the first two places on the grid. Senna was third fastest and Prost fifth fastest in 1m 29.175s, compared with Mansell's 1m 26.128s. Johansson, still getting to grips with the McLaren, was tenth fastest in 1m 30.476s. The race was to prove one of attrition and tyres. Initially Piquet pulled out a lead over Senna and Mansell. After only seven laps Piquet was in the pits for new tyres, but, more seriously, so the team could remove from the radiator ducts accumulated rubbish. During the first lap the wild Brazilian crowd had thrown showers of paper in the air, a fair quantity of which had been sucked into the ducts of the Williams. Piquet rejoined the race in 11th place and only four laps later Mansell stopped at the pits for the same reason as his team-mate. It seems that Williams had forgotten to take the very simple precaution, one followed frequently in the past, of fitting mesh guards to the front of the side pods. Senna led until the end of lap 13, but unhappy with the handling of his car, stopped at the pits, so that Prost assumed the lead. Prost, driving steadily and conserving his tyres, was to make two pit stops for tyres and apart from laps 17-20 he now led the race throughout to win from Piquet with Johansson third. Senna retired because of lubrication problems and Mansell fell back to finish sixth after a tyre punctured.

On his début with the McLaren team Stefan Johansson finished third in Brazil behind Prost and Piquet (Williams).

Alain Prost made a brilliant start to the 1987 season by winning the first round of the World Championship, the Brazilian Grand Prix at Rio de Janeiro, with the new MP4/3.

San Marino Grand Prix

The Imola race was marred by a crash during the first qualifying session when Piquet's Williams went out of control at the very fast Tambarello curve and hit the retaining wall. Piquet was badly concussed, but anxious to race, and only after protracted arguments, accepted that he was not fit. During Friday's qualifying three of McLaren's TAG engines blew up; the wrong chips had been used in the engine management system, resulting in the

engines running on a very lean mixture and suffering piston failures. Despite this, however, Prost took third place on the grid in 1m 26.135s behind Senna in pole
1m 25.826s and Mansell (1m 25.946s). Johansson was eighth fastest in 1m 28.708s.

The start was delayed because Brundell, Boutsen (Benetton) and Cheever (Arrows) all stalled and the length of the race was shortened by one lap to avoid wasting time topping up fuel tanks on the grid. Senna led initially, but then Mansell took the lead and on lap 5 Prost slipped into second place ahead of Senna. On lap 15 Prost's McLaren stopped out on the circuit because of alternator failure. Mansell won from Senna, Alboreto (Ferrari) and with Johansson in fourth place.

Although Prost retired early in the San Marino Grand Prix at Imola because of alternator failure, Johansson finished a strong third behind Mansell (Williams), Senna (Lotus) and Alboreto (Ferrari).

Belgian Grand Prix

There were minor aerodynamic changes to the McLarens at Spa-Francorchamps, including stiffer side-plates to the front wings, a result of a failure on Johansson's car at Imola. The Williams entries again dominated practice, and Mansell took pole in 1m 52.026s, with Piquet second, Senna third and Prost back in sixth place. Prost, who recorded 1m 54.186s, had been unhappy with the handling of his car. Johansson was tenth fastest in 1m 55.781s.

At the start Mansell led from Senna and Prost, but on that first lap Streiff lost control of his Tyrrell just after L'Eau Rouge and hit the barriers, with sufficient force to tear the Cosworth engine from the chassis. Team-mate Palmer topped the rise to find the monocoque of Streiff's car on the left of the track and the engine and transmission on the right. Palmer hit the monocoque of the crashed Tyrrell and Alliot stopped his Lola to help. The race was stopped immediately. Refuelling was allowed, the race would run the full distance from scratch when restarted and drivers would be allowed to use their spare cars (Berger and Boutsen had also collided on that first lap). The first lap of the restarted race was marred by a comparatively minor incident that was blown up into a major newspaper sensation. Senna made a superb start, heading Mansell. At the exit to the Pouhon corner, Mansell pulled alongside Senna on the inside and the Williams driver was on the line for the next corner. Mansell's right rear wheel contacted Senna's left front and the two cars spun off into the sand. Senna was unable to restart but Mansell rejoined at the end of the field and retired after 17 laps. Afterwards Mansell made his way to the Lotus pit where he grabbed Senna by the collar and had to be restrained by the Lotus mechanics from hitting the Brazilian. It was an incident that did the reputation of neither driver any good, but simply benefitted their rivals.

Piquet led for nine laps, but retired after bolts worked loose on the turbocharger, dropped out and caused the hot gases to melt a pipe; this resulted in the engine management system over-compensating and the Honda engine lost its performance. With

Piquet out, Prost took the lead ahead of Fabi (Benetton) and the steadily driving Johansson soon moved up into second place. So McLarens took first and second places, with Prost also setting fastest lap of 132.513 mph (1m 57.153s), ahead of de Cesaris (Brabham) and Cheever (Arrows).

Monaco Grand Prix

Practice resulted in Mansell fastest (1m 23.039s), ahead of Senna, Piquet and Prost (1m 25.083s), with Johansson seventh in 1m 26.317s. The McLarens had suffered minor problems in practices, but Prost's real complaint was the lack of power of the TAG engine compared with the Honda of the Williams. Johansson had a turbocharger failure during the untimed session on the Thursday, and he was reprimanded by the stewards for passing the scene of the collision between Alboreto (Ferrari) and Danner (Zakspeed) at undiminished speed – the young Swedish driver's response was that there had been no warning flags.

Work under way on the McLarens at Monaco in 1987.

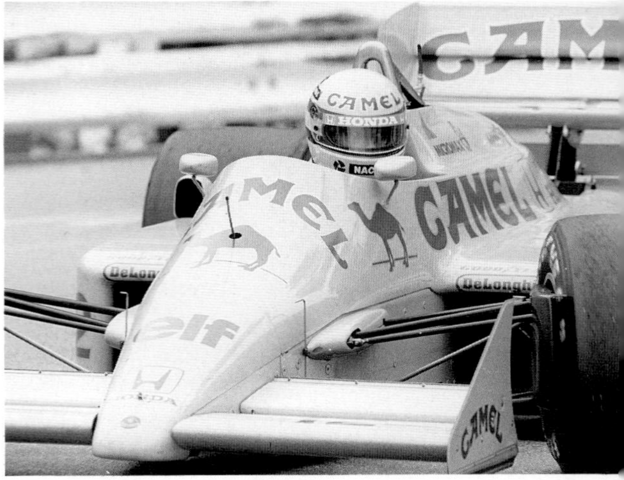

Ayrton Senna (Lotus 99T-Honda) scored a fine win at Monaco in 1987 after the retirement of Mansell's Williams and won again at Detroit.

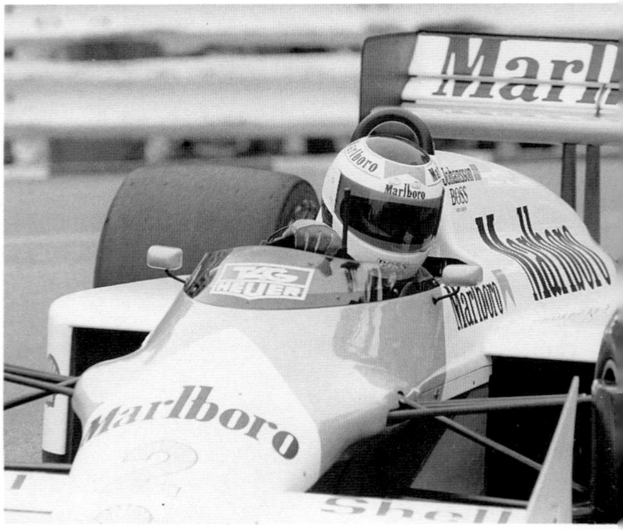

Monaco was a bad race for the McLaren team and both drivers retired. This is Johansson who was eliminated by engine trouble.

As he had dominated practice, so Mansell dominated much of the race leading for the first 30 laps until forced to retire because of loss of turbocharger boost pressure, the result of a fractured weld on an exhaust pipe. Senna took the lead, scoring a convincing victory ahead of Piquet. It was a particularly encouraging victory for Lotus who had been struggling to perfect the computer-controlled active suspension system used on the 99T.

The McLaren team had a thoroughly miserable race. Neither MP4/3 ran well from the start. Prost's car spent most of the race on five cylinders, but a spirited chase through the field brought him up to third place ahead of Alboreto (Ferrari), only to retire on lap 76, two laps before the finish, when the TAG engine blew up. He was eventually classified ninth, three laps in arrears. Johansson's McLaren was plagued by a bad misfire, and he struggled round at the tail of the field until the engine eventually failed.

United States Grand Prix (Detroit)

Minor changes to the McLarens included double rear wings and, on Prost's car, smaller turbochargers. On this tight and tortuous street circuit Mansell was fastest in 1m 39.264s, ahead of Senna (1m 40.607s), Piquet (1m 40.942s) and with Prost fifth in 1m 42.357s. Lack of grip plagued both McLarens, and poor Johansson complained most bitterly that there was no grip anywhere round the circuit. This accounted for his poor 11th place on the grid in 1m 43.797s.

Although on race morning there was low cloud and a damp track, it had dried out by the start of the race. Mansell made a superb start, accelerating away from Senna at a steady rate, with Piquet third, chased hard by Cheever (Arrows) and Prost back in seventh place at the end of the first lap. Whilst Mansell dominated the race in front, Prost was steadily climbing up through the field so that by lap 25 he was in third place. Mansell stopped for new tyres at the end of lap 34, an error because the tyres would have lasted the race, and his pit stop was delayed by at least ten seconds because of a jammed rear wheel nut. This elevated Prost to second place, but Mansell, driving like the very devil, caught and passed Prost within two laps and started to chase after Senna who had determined, on the basis of information received from his pit, as to the state of Mansell's discarded tyres, to continue non-stop. All this while, Piquet was fighting his way back through the field after a pit stop to change a punctured tyre and as Mansell slowed because of severe cramp, so Piquet moved further and further towards the front. Piquet displaced Prost for third place on lap 43, Mansell dropped back, and Piquet finished in second place, albeit over 34 seconds behind Senna, with Prost third, Berger (Ferrari) fourth, and Mansell fifth. Poor Johansson had a thoroughly miserable race, for he was delayed after a first lap incident when he had been pushed into the rear of Warwick (Arrows), shedding a front wing end plate. He later spent a long while in the pits because of an engine misfire that was cured by changing the electronic control box. At the end of the race he was seventh, three laps in arrears.

French Grand Prix

In 1987 the Canadian Grand Prix was cancelled and so after just one race on the western side of the Atlantic, the teams returned to Europe for the French Grand Prix held on the Paul Ricard circuit near Marseille. Although the days of the TAG engine were numbered, Porsche had continued development work and in France the McLarens ran engines with improved fuel consumption and greater power. Pole position again went to Mansell in 1m 06.454s, but Prost was second fastest in 1m 06.877s whilst Senna, desperately anxious to score a third successive victory, was third fastest in 1m 07.024s. Johansson took ninth place on the grid in 1m 08.577s, still not showing the form expected of him after his fine performances with Ferrari in 1985-86.

Nigel Mansell dominated the French race, only losing the lead when he stopped for new tyres at the end of lap 35 and dropped to third place behind Prost. On rejoining the race he quickly passed the McLaren and chased after Piquet whom he passed when the Brazilian made a rare error of judgement, running wide at the infield right-hand bend and allowing Mansell room to take the lead. Piquet chased Mansell hard for several laps, but then decided to stop for more new tyres – a major error, for he lost time when he stalled his engine, cancelling

In the 1987 French Grand Prix Alain Prost finished third, one of his better performances in a season that became less and less satisfactory for McLaren International.

out any advantage in lap times from new tyres, and eventually came back to finish second, just under eight seconds behind his team-mate. For Prost it had been a poor race, for although he had held third place in the opening laps and moved up to sixth when Piquet made his first pit stop for tyres, the combination of the power deficiency of the TAG engine and a worsening misfire as the race progressed, kept the French World Champion out of contention for the lead. He finished a distant third, over 55 seconds behind the winner, with Senna fourth; on this circuit the Lotus 99T, despite the same engine, was simply no match for the Williams. Johansson worked his way up to sixth place, only to retire because of a broken alternator belt, and was classified eighth.

British Grand Prix

Once again at Silverstone the Williams FW11Bs dominated practice and Piquet took pole position in 1m 07.110s, with Mansell second fastest in 1m 07.180s. The 'second runners', Lotus and McLaren, just lacked the power to get on even terms with the Williams entries; Senna was third on the grid and Prost fourth. Johansson was back in tenth place. Prost's qualifying had been interrupted by a number of minor problems, including a jamming throttle and a leaking turbocharger wastegate pipe.

For the second race in succession FW11Bs took the first two places. Piquet led for the first 62 laps of this 65 lap race, but on lap 63 Mansell, having just set fastest lap of the race and driven his Williams so hard that his fuel situation was critical, moved to the left on the approach to Stowe, Piquet moved left to cover him and Mansell, having 'sold the dummy' shot to the right and took the inside line into the corner. The two cars almost collided, Piquet backed off and Mansell had the lead and victory for the third time in 1987. Ayrton Senna, still heading the World Championship table, took third place, a lap in arrears. Mansell ran out of fuel on his slowing down lap. Neither of the McLarens finished this race. Prost was in a secure fourth place but the failure of a clutch bearing damaged a sensor on the engine control unit and the engine cut out. Johansson's race was soon over, for he was holding sixth place on lap 19 when the engine blew up in a big way and the rear end of his McLaren was enveloped in flames and smoke.

German Grand Prix

Further development by Porsche on the TAG engines increased power output without the expense of a loss in fuel economy. In practice Mansell took pole in 1m 42.616s, Senna was second in 1m 42.873s, but Prost was third on the grid in 1m 43.202s, ahead of Piquet. Johansson took eighth place in 1m 45.428s.

On the first lap Senna led from Mansell and Prost with Piquet fourth. Mansell passed Senna on lap 2 and Prost pushed through into second place on the same lap. On lap 8 Prost took the lead from Mansell, dropped to third place when he made his tyre change stop on lap 19, but quickly resumed the lead when the FW11Bs made their stops. Prost seemed assured of victory, but just over four laps from the chequered flag the McLaren coasted to a halt because of alternator belt failure. Mansell was already out of the race because of a seized engine, Senna made three quick pit stops, initially because the cockpit boost control had failed, then for a check, then again to have a damaged nose wing replaced which had not been noticed during the earlier stops. At the finish Piquet was the clear leader by nearly two minutes. Johansson took a fine second place, although on the last lap his right front tyre deflated, then disintegrated completely and he crossed the line with the wheel hanging off. Senna had driven a remarkable race despite all his problems and he finished third, a lap in arrears, although the only cars behind him were the normally aspirated Tyrrells of Streiff and Palmer and the Lola of Alliot.

Stefan Johansson finished second at Hockenheim, despite the right front wheel almost falling off because of a deflating tyre.

Hungarian Grand Prix

Because of the problems suffered at Hockenheim, the TAG turbo engines at the Hungaroring were fitted with new alternator drive belts (according to Porsche already planned prior to Prost's Hockenheim retirement). Because this was a slow circuit, the McLarens were again fitted with the double rear wings, just as they had used at Monaco. In practice Prost was fourth fastest in 1m 30.156s, with pole position going to Mansell in 1m 28.047s. Senna's Lotus proved no match in qualifying for the Williams opposition and he was in sixth place in 1m 30.387s, with the second McLaren of Johansson two places lower down the grid in 1m 31.228s. Once again Johansson was complaining bitterly about the lack of grip around the circuit.

Another third place for Prost followed in the Hungarian Grand Prix. Here Prost hustles second-place finisher Senna.

The race *should* have proved another Mansell benefit, for he took the lead at the start, ahead of the Ferraris of Berger and Alboreto, with Piquet fourth, Senna fifth and Prost back in sixth place. Johansson's race was soon over, for he spun wildly on lap 15, by when he was leading Prost, because of a seized differential. Prost was close enough to have a bad moment avoiding the spinning McLaren and he lost about ten seconds because of the incident. As the race progressed, so Prost climbed up through the field and by lap 59 of this 76-lap race he was in fourth place behind Mansell, Piquet and Senna. Six laps from the finish Mansell retired for the almost incredible reason that the right rear wheel nut had come undone, so permitting the wheel to work loose. Piquet, who also set fastest lap, won from Senna and Prost.

Austrian Grand Prix

Once again in Austria the Williams FW11Bs dominated practice with Piquet taking pole in 1m 23.357s, Mansell second fastest and both Senna and the McLaren drivers well down the grid. Senna was seventh fastest, Prost ninth. Johansson, after a most horrific practice accident, was 14th. During Friday's qualifying he came over the hill leading to the Jochen Rindt Kurve to be confronted by a deer on the track. The young Swedish driver was travelling at around 150 mph, swerved to avoid the deer but it struck the left front wheel of the McLaren, tearing off the wheel and suspension so that the McLaren totally out of control hit the barriers on the outside of the track. Johansson admitted to being very badly shaken and bruised. It was learned later that he had a cracked rib. It also became known that the deer had been running in the woods close to the track for some while, but that the officials had taken no steps whatsoever to bring practice to an end whilst the animal was dealt with.

Alain Prost on his way to sixth place in the Austrian Grand Prix.

In all there were three starts in Austria. As Brundell accelerated his Zakspeed off the line at the first start, the car veered to the left, hit the crash barriers, and whilst the field avoided Brundell, Campos (Minardi) and Ginzani (Ligier) collided, as did the Tyrrells of Streiff and Palmer. At the second start Mansell accelerated, but his Williams hesitated because of a clutch problem. For some inexplicable reason Berger also hesitated as he passed the Williams, Patrese veered to the right to avoid them both, collided with the Arrows of Cheever and was rammed by Johansson. Brundell ran into the back of Johansson's McLaren and the Brabham. Several other cars were involved in accidents and once again the race was stopped.

On the parade lap for the third start, Prost's engine refused to pick up and he stopped at the end of the pit lane. This meant that he had to start from the pit lane, along with four other drivers who had all missed the grid because of frantic work on their cars to repair damage incurred in the second start. The queue in the pit lane was joined by Alboreto whose steering wheel had not been put on straight and who had pulled off for this to be sorted out.

At the end of the first lap Piquet led from Boutsen (Benetton), Berger, Mansell, Fabi (Benetton) and Patrese with Johansson in ninth place and Prost desperately fighting his way up through the field. Mansell, whose clutch had recovered after the second start, gradually worked his way through to hold second place behind Piquet, and once again the

FW11Bs took the first two places. Prost rose to third place, but an electrical fault had meant that none of the instruments were working and his car lost power towards the end of the race. He eventually took sixth place, two laps in arrears, behind the Benettons of Fabi and Boutsen and Senna's fifth-place Lotus. Johansson finished seventh.

Italian Grand Prix

Despite testing at Imola shortly before the Italian Grand Prix on the much faster Monza circuit, there were no important changes to the McLarens. As the season progressed, the faster circuits featured more, so McLaren slipped down the list of serious contenders. At Monza Piquet and Mansell took the first two places on the grid, Prost was fifth fastest and Johansson was back in 11th place. The race proved yet another Williams benefit with Piquet winning at 144.553 mph, from Senna and his team-mate Mansell. Johansson, still suffering from a broken rib, did well to finish sixth, but it was a bad race for Prost. Early in the race his McLaren developed an engine misfire and although he was fifth at the end of the first four laps, pit stops caused him to drop down the field to eventually finish 15th, four laps in arrears.

Nelson Piquet, winner of the 1987 Italian Grand Prix and that year's World Championship.

Portuguese Grand Prix

Following the Italian Grand Prix, McLaren conducted a test session at Monza and this had resulted in a number of electronic changes. At Estoril practice was dominated by Berger who took pole position in 1m 17.620s, with Mansell and Piquet second and fourth, but Prost was third fastest in 1m 17.994s. Johansson was in eighth place in 1m 20.134s.

It was to prove a bad race for the Williams team and a good race for McLaren and Ferrari. Although Mansell led at the end of the first lap, he was soon passed by the Austrian Ferrari driver who remained in front for much of the rest of the race. Mansell retired because of electronic problems after 13 laps and Prost had moved up into second place behind Berger. When Berger spun just over two laps before the finish because of worn tyres, Prost slipped into the lead, Berger recovered and so the finishing order was Prost – Berger – Piquet – Fabi – Johansson. In the World Championship Nelson Piquet was now the clear leader with 67 points, to the 49 of Ayrton Senna, 43 of Nigel Mansell and 40 of Alain Prost.

Spanish Grand Prix

So the season continued, with Williams domination and the McLarens always to the fore but rarely race winners. At the Jerez circuit Piquet and Williams again dominated qualifying, with Piquet taking pole position in 1m 22.461s, Mansell second fastest, followed by the two Ferraris, Senna, Fabi (Benetton) and then Prost in seventh place in 1m 24.596s. Johansson was two places further back on the grid with a time of 1m 26.147s. Qualifying was ruined for the McLaren team by handling problems that had been getting worse all season and in Prost's case, accompanied by an engine misfire. During Friday's qualifying Prost was forced to spin his car when the TAG turbo engine cut out without warning.

Mansell led throughout the race, with Piquet,

At Monza Alain Prost trailed home in 15th position after delays caused by an engine misfire, while Johansson, seen here, finished sixth.

The signalling board says it all – in the 1987 Portuguese Grand Prix at Estoril McLaren International bounced back and Prost won the race from Berger (Ferrari).

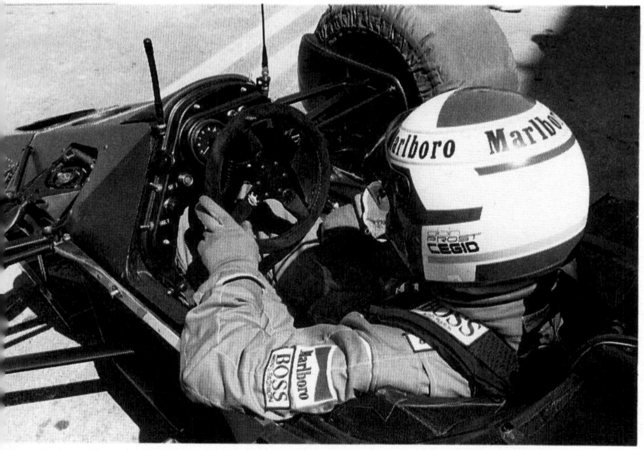

Stefan Johansson in the pits at the 1987 Spanish Grand Prix at Jerez.

responding badly to pressure as World Championship leader, driving erratically to finish fourth. As the race progressed, Prost, who finished the first lap in ninth place worked his way up through the field, benefitting from the retirement of the Ferraris, to take second place with Johansson third. Senna, who had driven throughout the race without a stop for a tyre change and for many laps had held up faster drivers, finished fifth.

Mexican Grand Prix

At the Hermanos Rodriguez Autodrome McLaren used larger turbochargers to compensate for the altitude (7,200 feet), larger radiators and the onboard computer had been modified necessitating an aerial on the dash panel. Mansell took pole position in 1m 18.383s, but at this race the supremacy of the Williams FW11Bs was challenged by Berger who was second fastest in qualifying in 1m 18.426s. Prost was fifth fastest in 1m 18.742s, whilst Johansson had another disastrous practice. He suffered engine failures on both qualifying days and had to switch to Prost's spare car halfway through the final qualifying session. His 15th place on the grid reflected his fortunes but not his talent. On only the first lap of the race Prost was eliminated when he was chopped by Piquet who had braked hard, forcing Prost to veer to the right locking his brakes, and both cars spun off. Prost's race was over, but Piquet was given a push-start and rejoined in 25th place. A lap later Johansson spun, to avoid a collision between Nakajima (Lotus) and Warwick (Arrows), and was rammed by Danner's Zakspeed. In the meanwhile Boutsen led with his Benetton from Berger, but the final finishing order was Williams first and second, with Mansell leading Piquet across the line. Patrese (Brabham) finished third ahead of Cheever (Arrows) and Fabi (Benetton).

At Jerez Johansson finished third behind Mansell (Williams) and team-mate Prost.

Alain Prost at the 1987 Japanese Grand Prix at Suzuka. He finished a poor seventh.

Japanese Grand Prix

The Japanese Grand Prix was introduced to the calendar for the first time after an interval of ten years at the Suzuka circuit at Shiroka which replaced the former Fuji circuit. On this sweeping and diving circuit the McLarens handled superbly and for the first time in 1987 Prost was on the front row of the grid, second fastest in 1m 40.652s, compared with Berger's pole in 1m 40.042s. Johansson was ninth fastest in 1m 43.371s. Mansell had spun into a tyre barrier during Friday's qualifying and was too badly bruised to take part in the race. Berger led throughout, but although Prost held second place at the end of the first lap, he ran over some debris from Alliot's Lola that had been pushed into the pit wall by Arnoux's Ligier at the start. This punctured the McLaren's left rear tyre and he had to nurse the car around the full length of the circuit before a new tyre could be fitted. This cost him two laps and put him completely out of contention. Johansson had one of the best races of the season, coming through to hold second place, but his fuel level was critical, he was passed by Senna and pushed back into third place on the very last lap. Prost finished seventh, a lap in arrears, having established a Formula 1 record for the circuit at 126.21 mph.

In his last race for McLaren – Stefan Johansson in the 1987 Australian Grand Prix at Adelaide. He was eliminated by brake problems.

Australian Grand Prix

The Adelaide race was to prove another Ferrari benefit. Berger took pole position in practice in 1m 17.267s (Prost was second in 1m 17.967s) and he led throughout the race to score his second successive win of the season. Senna finished second on the road but was disqualified because his car was found to have oversized brake ducts at the post-race scrutineering and this elevated the other Ferrari of Michele Alboreto to second place in the results. Although Prost drove a steady race holding second place at one stage, his race came to an end when the right front brake locked up and he spun into the tyre barriers. Already Johansson had retired for the same reason.

Nelson Piquet took the World Championship with 73 points to 61 of his team-mate Nigel Mansell, with Senna third with 57 points and Prost fourth with 46. Williams's domination of the Constructors' Cup was complete with a total of 137 points to the 76 of McLaren. The impression that McLaren's fortunes were on the wane was to be dissipated in 1988.

Stefan Johansson, previously with Ferrari, joined Alain Prost in the McLaren team in 1987.

1987

In the Belgian Grand Prix at Spa-Francorchamps Stefan Johansson (MP4/3) leads Christian Danner (Zakspeed). The young Swedish driver finished second behind team-mate Prost.

Just after the second start of the 1987 Belgian Grand Prix Alain Prost leads Thierry Boutsen (Benetton B187) and the rest of the field through Eau Rouge. The leaders Nelson Piquet (Williams) and Michele Alboreto (Ferrari F1/87) have already disappeared towards Radillon. Prost won the race, a notable victory for it now meant that he had equalled Jackie Stewart's record of 27 Grand Prix wins.

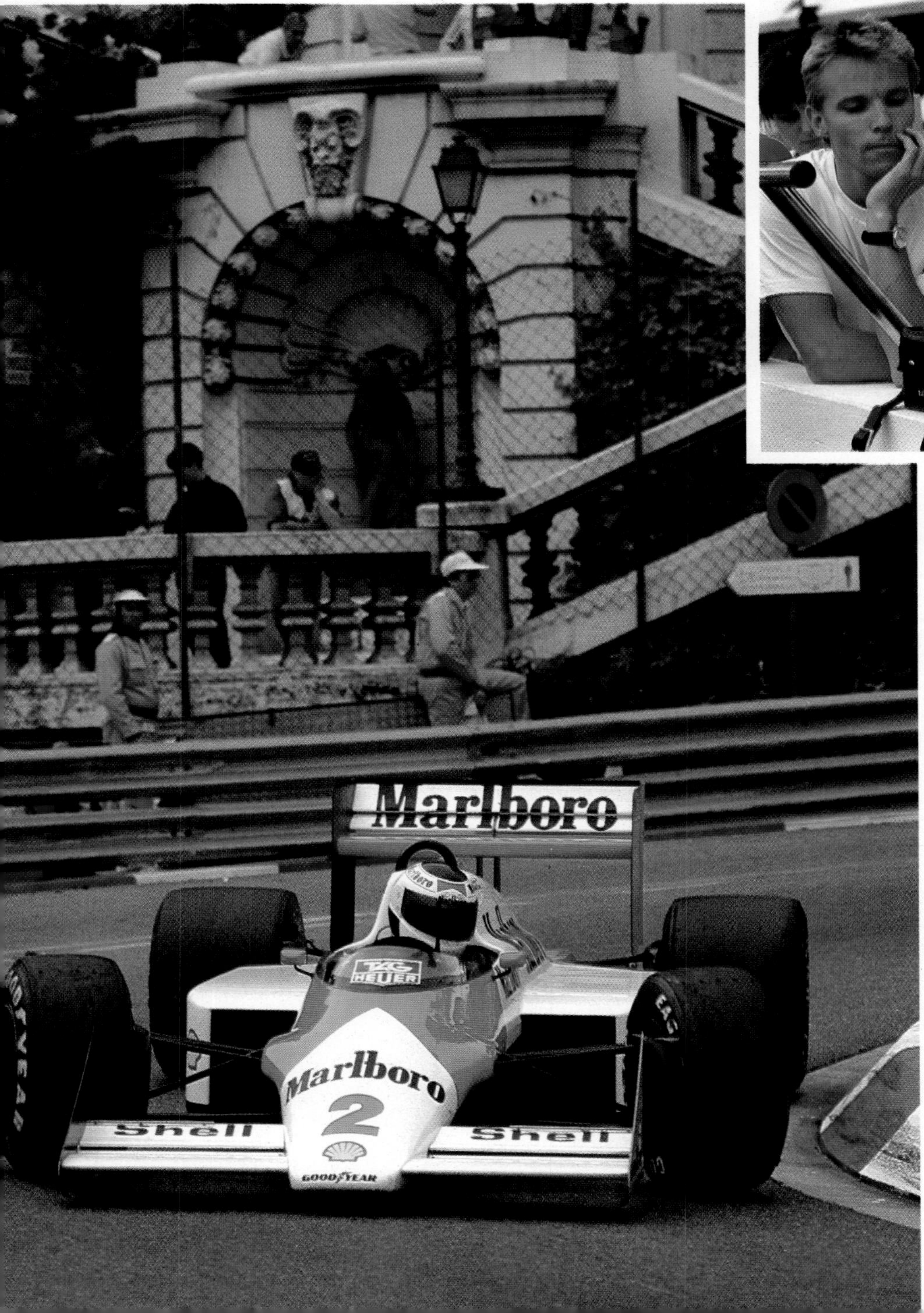

Stefan Johansson during qualifying for the 1987 Monaco Grand Prix. In the race he was slowed by an electrical problem that caused a misfire and engine trouble caused his eventual retirement.

Johansson watches practice times at the 1987 British Grand Prix.

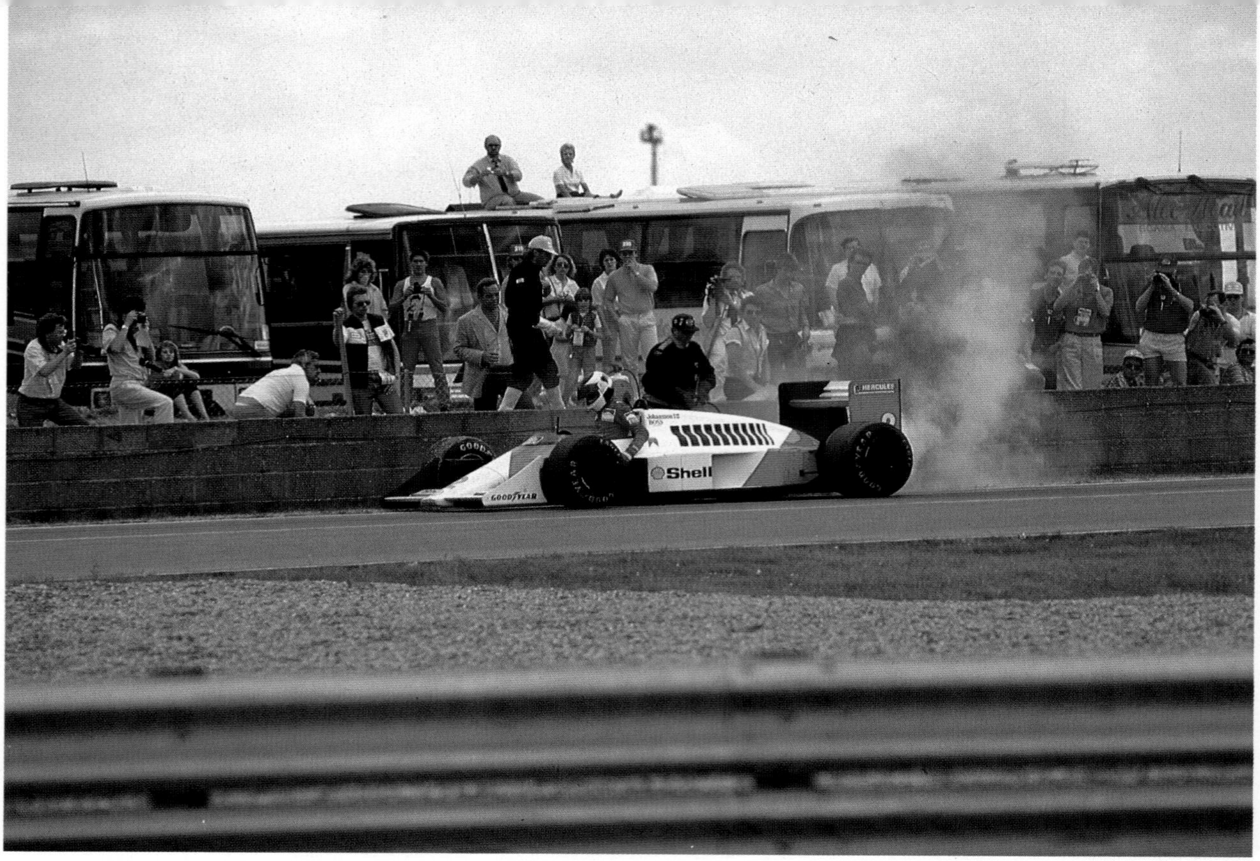

Above: In the British race Johansson retired because of a turbocharger fire.

Right: Alain Prost's pit stop for tyres in the German Grand Prix. The alternator drive belt broke a little over four laps from the finish and he was classified seventh.

Ayrton Senna, who joined McLaren International from Lotus for the 1988 season. This photograph of Senna in JPS overalls was taken in 1986.

1988

Pit stop for Alain Prost with the new MP4/4 in the 1988 Brazilian Grand Prix. He won the race, but Senna was disqualified because of a minor infringement.

Right: At Monaco in 1988 Senna, seen here, was eliminated by a crash. He touched the crash barrier on the inside of the track at Portier, lost control and hit the barrier on the other side.

Below: Senna leads Prost and the Ferraris of Berger and Alboreto in the 1988 Belgian Grand Prix at Spa-Francorchamps. Senna and Prost took first and second places and both Ferraris retired.

The turbocharged V6 Honda RA168-E engine installed in the 1988 MP4/4 chassis.

The pull-rod front suspension of the MP4/4.

The push-rod rear suspension and longitudinal gearbox of the MP4/4.

Ayrton Senna at the 1988 Hungarian Grand Prix. Senna won the race by the narrowest of margins from team-mate Prost.

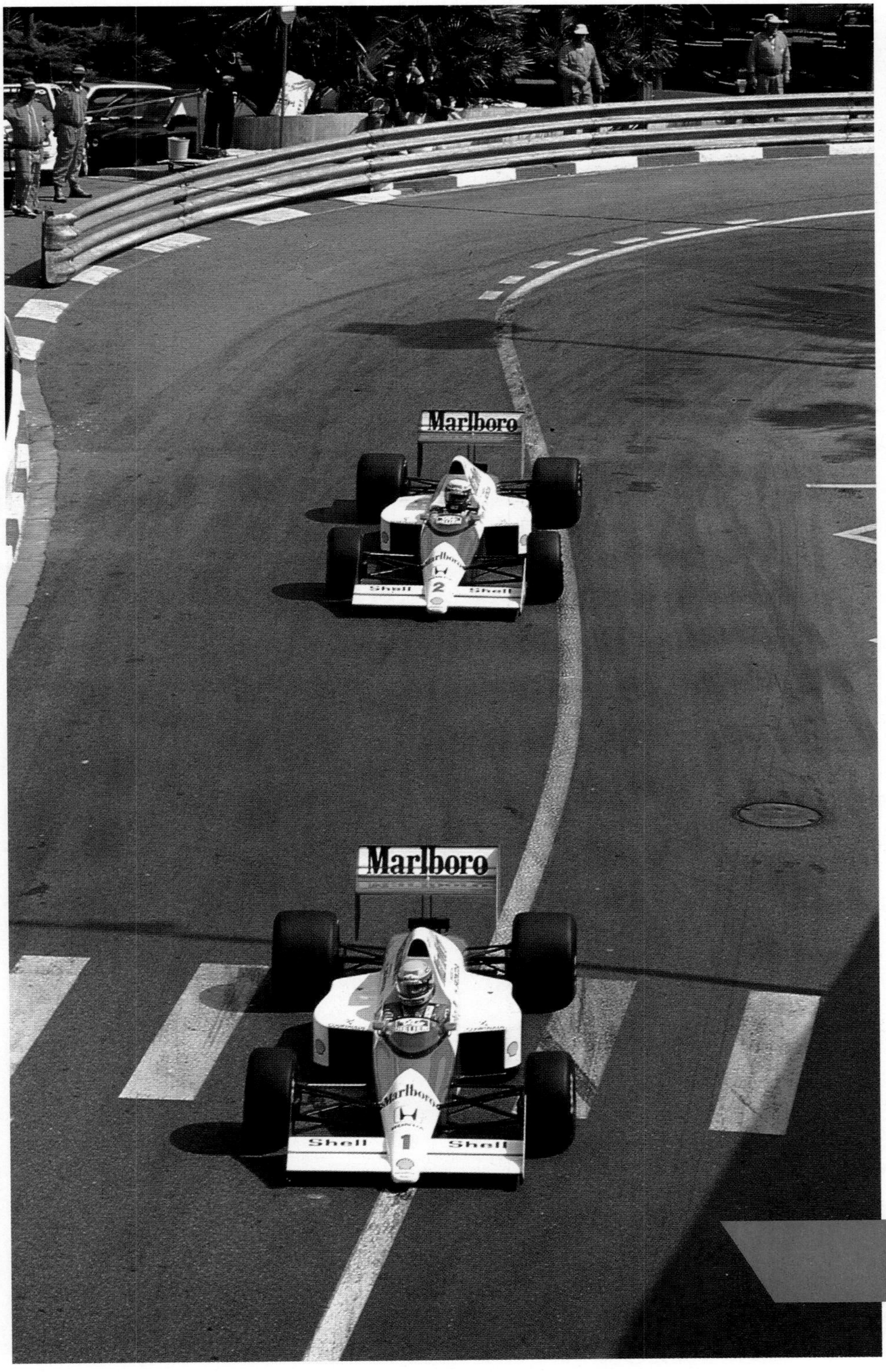

At Monaco in 1989 Senna and Prost took the first two places, but the Frenchman dispirited his supporters by offering no serious challenge to his Brazilian team-mate.

1989

Above: Senna and Prost in the 1989 Mexican Grand Prix on the Hermanos Rodriguez circuit in which they took the first two places. For the race, Honda prepared special engines adapted to the high altitude at which the race took place. In all there were five different versions of the V10 RA109E engine in 1990.

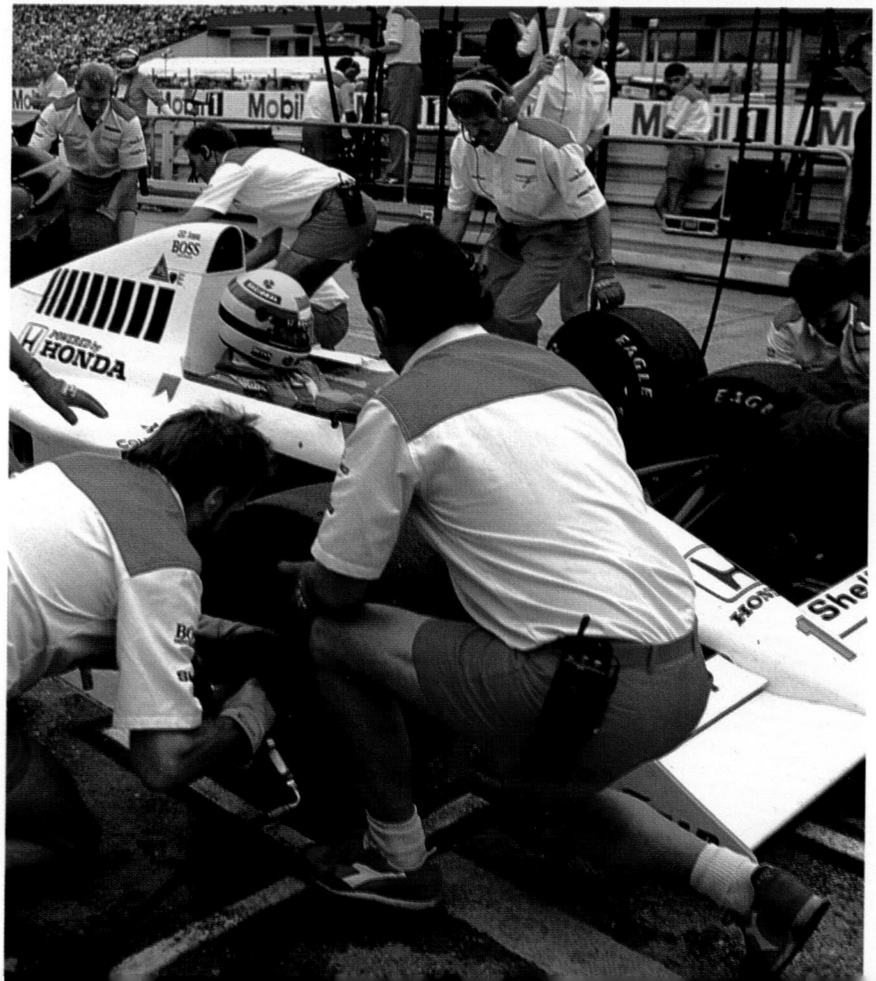

Right: At the German Grand Prix at Hockenheim Ayrton Senna makes a pit stop. Once again the McLarens took the first two places.

The old and the new: Alain Prost (above) seen at Suzuka won the 1989 Japanese Grand Prix and the controversial 1989 World Championship, but this was his last race for the team; he withdrew from the Australian race and has now joined Ferrari. Gerhard Berger (seen below) left Ferrari at the end of 1989 to drive for McLaren.

Gerhard Berger tyre testing with the MP4/5 at Estoril in December 1989.

Ayrton Senna remained with Marlboro McLaren in 1990, although there were fears at one time that he would not be allowed to compete in the 1990 World Championship. He is seen in the first round of the Championship at Phoenix which he won from Alesi (Tyrrell).

7: 1988: Almost Complete Domination

During 1987 dramatic changes had taken place that would materially enhance McLaren's prospects. Very shortly after the German Grand Prix Ayrton Senna's lawyers wrote to the Lotus team manager, Peter Warr, informing him that Senna would be operating the release clause in his contract with Lotus and moving to another team for 1988. Lotus then signed up Nelson Piquet, unhappy at Williams because the team would not regard him as the designated No.1 driver.

Once Piquet and Honda's favourite, Satorou Nakajima, had been signed up for 1988, Lotus was ensured that it would retain the use of Honda engines. Already the word was being passed that Williams, despite dominating much of the year's racing, and in fact to win the World Championship with Piquet, and having another year of their contract with Honda to run, would lose the supply of Honda engines at the end of 1987. It was soon known that Senna would be going to McLaren and before the Italian Grand Prix it was also known that McLaren would be the other Honda engine user in 1988. In fact Honda were to look upon McLaren as the premier team, as Lotus slipped further and further in the results. This of course meant the end of the TAG engine that McLaren had been using since the latter part of 1983. Many other uses for the TAG engine concept had been projected, but none of these went any further, even a proposal to use it as a helicopter engine. It was a sad end after so many years of development work on what had been a very successful design.

For 1988 Steve Nichols produced his first own design for McLaren, a logical development of the MP4/3, but with a much more reclined driving position that appeared to imitate the Brabham BT55, a very short fuel tank, revised rear bodywork with improved aerodynamics and a new three-axis gearbox designed by David North which stepped up the drive from the low-crankshaft line of the Honda V6 engine. Major change in the regulations had been the FISA decisions to limit turbocharger boost to 2.5 bars and fuel tank capacity to 150 litres.

By 1988 the face of Formula 1 was gradually changing in the light of the decision that the turbocharged formula would come to an end that year and that only normally aspirated 3500 cc cars would be permitted from 1989 onwards. More and more teams were running 3500 cc cars, including Williams which, following the loss of Honda, had adopted the Judd engine and the main opposition throughout 1988 was to come from the turbocharged Ferraris.

As a team, Prost and Senna were to prove an overwhelmingly strong combination, although their private relationship steadily disintegrated as the year progressed. After just a year with McLaren, poor Stephan Johansson was out in the cold and forced to take a drive with Ligier, as a result of which he was demoted from being a front runner to scrambling for a place on the back of the grid.

Brazilian Grand Prix

It was only 11 days prior to the race at Rio de Janeiro that the new MP4/4 ran in public for the first time at Imola and so impressive were the lap times of both Senna and Prost, that it was clear that McLaren were likely to regain their supremacy of four years previously. At Rio Senna took pole position in 1m 28.096s, whilst Mansell with the normally aspirated Williams was second on the grid in 1m 28.632s, with Prost third fastest in 1m 28.782s.

When the cars set off on the parade lap, Senna was motoring at a crawl – his McLaren had jammed in first gear. He brought the McLaren on to the grid and then raised his arms so as to delay the start. His car was pushed away from the grid and he took over the spare with a view to starting from the pit lane. Prost accelerated alongside Mansell and into the lead as the cars approached the first right-hand corner, and he remained in front throughout the race, building up an advantage when both Berger and Piquet, in second and third places, made second stops for tyres. Senna fought his way through the field to hold second place, but ever since the race had started Ron Dennis had been arguing with the race officials as to whether or not the Brazilian should be disqualified. The stewards' argument was that the race had been delayed as opposed to stopped and restarted, so Senna was in breach of the rules by changing to his spare car after the green flag had been shown. The argument that drivers should not be allowed to race on for lap after lap whilst disqualification is pending can be countered by the argument that most of these laps are spent by the team manager arguing with the stewards over their decision. At the finish Prost was just under nine seconds ahead of Berger (Ferrari) with Piquet (Lotus 100T) in third place.

San Marino Grand Prix

Prost had a new car, MP4/4-4 at Imola, which replaced chassis 3 written off by Senna during testing at Monza. This featured a revised surround to the cockpit and a stiffened front bulkhead. Senna and Prost took first two places in practice (Senna's pole was in 1m 27.148s). Senna led throughout the race, and once Prost had passed Piquet on lap 8 the McLarens were unchallenged for the first two places. Piquet with the less competitive Honda-powered Lotus had to fight for his third place very hard, fending off first Mansell, then the Benettons of Nannini and Boutsen.

Monaco Grand Prix

The McLaren band wagon rolled on at Monaco where Senna (1m 23.998s) and Prost (1m 25.425s) took first and second places on the grid ahead of the Ferraris of Berger and Alboreto. Whilst Senna made a brilliant start and steadily pulled out a lead at the head of the field, Prost was pushed back into third place by Berger and had to fight bitterly, trying again and again to snatch second place. It was not until lap 54 that he managed to draw alongside the Ferrari as they passed the end of the pits and slip into the lead. Whilst Senna had eased off, Prost was racing hard, and as soon as Senna was informed by the McLaren pit of the lessening gap between the two, he speeded up, setting a new lap record in 1m 26.321s (86.242 mph). Prost's response was to ease back to lapping at a rather more leisurely 1m 29s and Senna eased off as well, possibly believing that the race was in the bag and relaxing just a little too much. On lap 67 Senna touched the inside of the crash barrier at Portier, the steering wheel was jolted from his hands and despite standing on the brakes he ran into the barrier on the opposite side of the trade. At the finish Prost was the comfortable winner, over 20 seconds ahead of the Ferrari of Berger, with Alboreto's Ferrari in third place.

Mexican Grand Prix

At Mexico City the McLarens ran with larger turbochargers to compensate for the altitude at which the race was run. Almost inevitably Senna took pole in 1m 17.468s, with Prost second fastest in 1m 18.097s. Behind them came Berger, Piquet and Alboreto. Prost made a superb start, heading into a lead which he kept throughout the 67 laps of this race, while Senna, slowed by the unexpected and inexplicable tripping of his pop-off valve, made a slow start but picked up ground to snatch second place back from Piquet, and he held that position until the finish. Prost also set fastest lap in 1m 18.608s (125.807 mph). The Ferraris of Berger and Alboreto again took third and fourth places.

Ayrton Senna in the 1988 Monaco Grand Prix in which he was eliminated by a collision with the barrier.

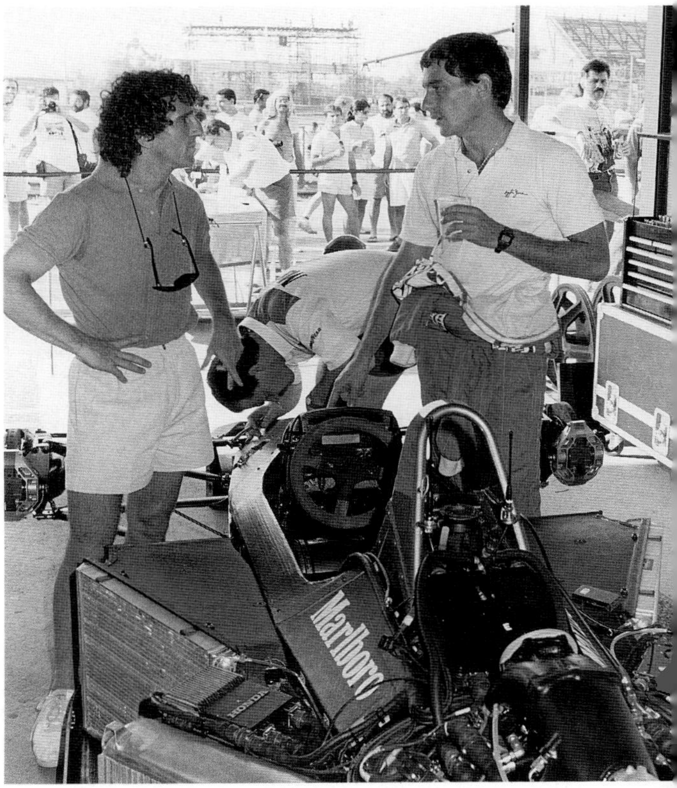

Alain Prost and Ayrton Senna, still on good terms, at the 1988 Brazilian Grand Prix shortly after the start of their long and stormy relationship.

Senna watches practice times at Mexico City.

At Mexico City Prost and Senna took the first two places.

In the Canadian Grand Prix Prost and Senna lead the Ferraris of Berger and Alboreto. Senna and Prost finished first and second in that order.

Canadian Grand Prix

At Montreal the power superiority of the McLarens was demonstrated once again and in practice only the Ferraris proved themselves still to be the best of the rest. Senna again took pole in 1m 21.681s, with Prost second on the grid in 1m 21.863s, with the second row occupied by the Ferraris of Berger and Alboreto. At the drivers' briefing Senna queried why pole position was on the right of the track, when the first bend was a left-hander. He was also concerned because he would have to start in the dirt off the racing line. The organisers were having none of it, claiming that the first right-hand gentle curve was in his favour. As expected, Prost headed off into the lead, followed by Senna and in the early laps of the race the two Honda-powered cars set such a fast pace that many observers wondered whether, in this one of the longest of the year's races, their fuel would last the distance. Senna surged into the lead on lap 19 when Prost was briefly baulked by a back-marker, both drivers in accordance with pit instructions turned down their turbocharge boost and they took the first two places. After the retirement of both Ferraris, third place went to the Benetton of Boutsen, with Piquet's Lotus fourth.

United States Grand Prix (Detroit)

Senna again took pole (1m 40.606s). Alongside him on the grid was Berger in 1m 41.464s, Alboreto was third fastest and Prost, far from happy, was back in fourth place in 1m 42.019s. On the Saturday there was to be a press conference for the winner of pole position but Senna failed to appear, and Ron Dennis insisted to the press that the team's technical de-briefing session was more important and that in any event 'we are trying to make history; you are only reporting it'.

When the starting light turned green, Senna was away first and just managed to hold off Berger into turn one, Alboreto was third and at the end of the lap Prost was back in fifth place. Senna led throughout and on lap 6 Prost moved up into second place. These remained the positions for the rest of the race. Berger was eliminated by Boutsen whose Benetton's right front wing plate slashed one of the Austrian's tyres forcing him to abandon the Ferrari out on the circuit; the other Benetton driver, Nannini, shunted Alboreto into a spin, causing him to drop right down the field. At the finish Boutsen was third and fourth place went to de Cesaris (Rial).

French Grand Prix

It almost goes without saying that McLaren was so satisfied with the performance of the cars in 1988 that there were no changes when they appeared at

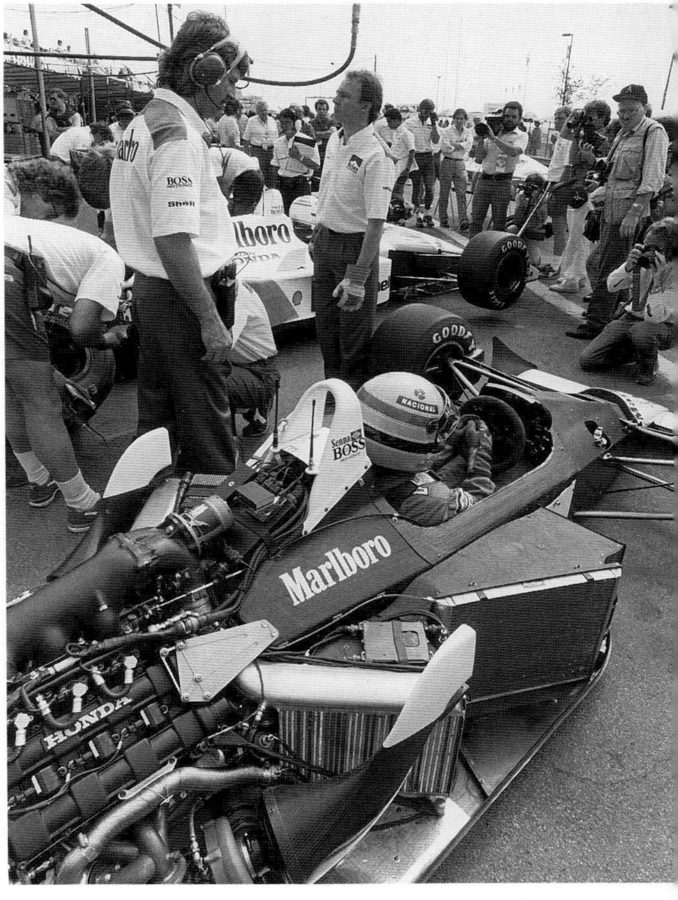

The McLaren pit at Detroit in 1988.

Two views of Prost in the 1988 Detroit Grand Prix. In the right hand column photograph he is passing the abandoned Arrows of Derek Warwick.

the Paul Ricard circuit. Inevitably the McLarens dominated qualifying, with Prost taking pole in 1m 07.589s, and Senna in second place in 1m 08.067s. Ferrari again were the 'best of the rest' and Berger and Alboreto occupied the second row of the grid. This was Prost's first pole position in two years and on his home circuit he was at the peak of his form, aggressive and willing to fight hard against his young and brilliant team-mate who was trying to topple him from his position of supremacy. The McLarens led throughout the race with Prost crossing the line first at an average of 116.495 mph, followed by Senna just over 30 seconds in arrear, slowed by gearbox problems, without which he would undoubtedly have been able to put up a better challenge to the reigning World Champion. The Ferraris took third and fourth places.

British Grand Prix

During the French race Senna had hit a kerb with his McLaren and the impact had made a large hole in the underside of the monocoque. To replace the damaged car McLaren completed chassis No.5 in time for the Silverstone race. In qualifying at Silverstone not only were the McLaren drivers, but most of the onlookers, astonished by the performance of the Ferraris and Berger (1m 10.133s) and Alboreto took the first two places on the grid ahead of Senna (1m 10.616s) and Prost (1m 10.736s).

It was raining heavily when the race started and intermittent rain fell throughout. When the green light came on, Berger moved into the lead ahead of Alboreto with Senna third; Senna forced his way past Alboreto, tried to overtake Berger, but the Austrian shut the door as Senna tried to push through on the inside into Stowe. It was not until lap 14 that Senna, well aware that Berger was setting an unrealistically fast pace in the bad conditions, passed the Ferrari driver on the inside at the exit of Abbey Curve. Whilst Senna pulled well ahead, both Berger and Alboreto were forced to turn down the boost on their turbochargers to conserve enough fuel to finish the race. As for Prost, he made a bad start, unhappy with the carbon clutch in the wet, finished the first lap in 11th place and fell further back down the field until, thoroughly unhappy with the handling of his car in these conditions, he decided to retire at the end of lap 24. As the race progressed so Berger slowed and the finishing order behind Senna after this 65-lap race was Mansell (Williams), Nannini (Benetton) and Gugelmin (March).

German Grand Prix

At Hockenheim it was back to the familiar pattern with Senna taking pole position in 1m 44.596s, Prost second fastest in 1m 44.873s and the two Ferraris third and fourth fastest. It was to prove another miserable race, cold and with intermittent drizzle and a wet track throughout. At the start Senna accelerated hard into the lead, but Prost made a bad start, spinning his wheels, and he finished the first lap back in fourth place. By lap 12 Prost had risen to second place behind his Brazilian team-mate, but any hopes of catching him were lost when he touched a kerb on lap 35 and spun. At the finish Senna was 11 seconds ahead of Prost who was far from happy in these conditions. The Ferraris of Berger and Alboreto took third and fourth places.

Hungarian Grand Prix

At the Hungaroring Senna was back in the car he had damaged in the French Grand Prix. At the eighth race in 1988, out of the ten so far held in the Championship, Senna took pole position, in 1m 27.635s, with Mansell (Williams) second fastest in 1m 27.743s. Prost who had a miserable time during the first day's qualifying, with electrical failure on the spare car, and then what he described as 'terrible understeer on his race car' finished qualifying a disappointed seventh in 1m 28.778s.

In the 1988 Hungarian Grand Prix Ayrton Senna leads the Williams of Nigel Mansell. Senna won the race, but Mansell retired because of exhaustion.

Senna accelerated away at the green light, but Mansell dogged his exhausts, with Patrese third and Prost back in ninth place. Gradually Senna extended his lead over Mansell, whilst Prost fought his way through the field. On lap 12 Mansell hit a kerb, spun and carried on in fourth place behind Patrese and Boutsen (Benetton). By lap 32 Prost had risen to third place behind Boutsen and he moved into second place on lap 47. Now Prost closed gradually on the leader, moving briefly into the lead on lap 49, but Senna passed him again on the same lap. During the last 15 laps of this 76-lap race, Prost was forced to ease back because of a front wheel vibration, and it was only in the closing laps that he realised the cause, debris picked up by the tyres when he had slid on to the dirt as he had fought his way past Senna on lap 49. Prost closed up on Senna again, but it was too late and he crossed the line less than a second on arrears. Prost and Senna were now joint first in the World Championship with 66 points to the 28 of Gerhard Berger in third place. In the Contructors' Cup McLaren led with 132 points to the 44 of Ferrari.

Belgian Grand Prix

Round 11 of the World Championship, with both drivers equal on points, was to be the turning point in the season, and on the Spa-Francorchamps circuit Prost had to defeat the young Brazilian if he was to have any serious hopes of winning the World Championship. At this circuit changes to the cars were few, although the MP4/4s featured modified steering geometry pick-up points, at lower positions on the front suspension uprights, and, on this fast circuit, smaller rear wings. Neither of the McLaren drivers were completely happy in qualifying, for Senna never had a clear run, and Prost was complaining that on the Friday the Honda engine was dying when he made downward gear changes. Because of drizzle on the Saturday, the Friday qualifying times determined positions on the grid. Inevitably, or almost so, Senna took pole in 1m 53.718s, Prost second fastest and with Alboreto fourth in 1m 55.665s.

If qualifying was to be two-car two-team battle, so were the results of the race to prove not only another demonstration of McLaren domination, but

Alain Prost in the 1988 Belgian Grand Prix in which he took second place.

with the Benettons performing solidly and finishing well up the field in formation. Prost led away at the green light, whilst Senna, using too much throttle, had a little too much wheel spin, followed through in second place and overtook at Les Combes. Senna and Prost led throughout the race and Senna won at an average of 126.415 mph. Prost's second place however had not been unchallenged, for Berger was right alongside McLaren under braking for Les Combes at the end of the second lap, but he had problems with his engine management system and although he set fastest lap of the race, both Ferraris retired. At the finish third and fourth places went to Boutsen and Nannini with their Benettons.

Italian Grand Prix

On this high speed circuit the grid represented a mirror image of that at Spa (at Spa pole position is on the right and at Monza on the left) and at the Italian circuit Senna took pole in 1m 25.974s, with Prost in second place in 1m 26.277s, and with Berger and Alboreto third and fourth fastest. Changes to the McLaren were limited to strengthened steering arm pick-up points on the front suspension uprights, two-piece rear wings and larger turbocharger ducts. Initially the race followed the expected pattern but perhaps at Monza Ron

Ayrton Senna, seen here leading Nannini (Benetton) was eliminated in the 1988 Italian Grand Prix by a collision with Schlesser (Williams) and the race was won by Berger (Ferrari).

Dennis was to rue his statement that McLaren was 'making history', for the history that he had wanted to make was a clean sweep of all 16 races by the team during the year. McLaren's failure at Monza was to destroy any chance of creating that record, a record that had never been achieved since the inception of the World Championship in 1950.

Inevitably Senna and Prost led away from the start and their domination seemed complete until Prost retired with engine trouble in the pits at the end of lap 35. This allowed the Ferraris of Berger and Alboreto to move up into second and third places, but Senna had a commanding lead. As the race progressed, so Berger began to speed up and close on Senna and, by the end of lap 49 of this 51-lap race, Berger had reduced the deficiency to 4.9 seconds. As they approached the chicane on that lap, Jean Schlesser, in 11th place as substitute driver for Williams, moved over to the extreme right, to allow Senna to lap him for the second time. For some unaccountable reason, the Williams locked its brakes at the edge of the track and slid straight on, while Senna who had not left enough room, collided with the Williams, with the right-rear wheel of the McLaren bouncing over the left-front of the Williams. The McLaren spun to a halt, wedged on top of a kerb, whilst Schlesser carried on to finish 11th and Berger swept past into the lead. Berger and Alboreto took the first and second places ahead of the Arrows of Cheever and Warwick. It may have been the only chink in the supremacy of McLaren during 1988, but it was the success that the *Tifosi* so desperately wanted to witness on home ground.

Portuguese Grand Prix

At Estoril there was a new chassis, No.6, for Prost. There was also a change in the pattern of domination seen in 1988, for, only for the second time in 1988, Prost took pole position in 1m 17.411s, with Senna second fastest in 1m 17.869s. The growing power of the normally aspirated March 881s was demonstrated by Capelli who was third fastest on the grid in 1m 18.812s ahead of Berger. Senna and Prost accelerated off the line fighting hard for the first corner, with Senna coming out ahead of the Frenchman, but behind them Warwick had stalled, de Cesaris had run into the Arrows and Sala (Minardi) and Nakajima (Lotus) were involved in the same accident. The race was stopped and restarted 15 minutes later. Once again Senna and Prost accelerated into the lead, with Senna firmly pushing across Prost into the first corner. Once again Prost was in fighting mood and on the pit straight drew alongside the Brazilian, refusing to back off when Senna veered to the right and forced his way through into the lead at 180 mph. Prost led for the remainder of the race, with Senna sixth after a collision with Mansell.

In the 1988 Spanish Grand Prix Ayrton Senna leads Riccardo Patrese (Williams), Ivan Capelli (March), and Alessandro Nannini (Benetton). Senna finished fourth in this race and ran out of fuel at the last corner after the start/finish line.

Spanish Grand Prix

The only changes to the McLarens at Jerez were the adoption of single-plane rear wings (the only other team to use these was Lola) and the two race cars were fitted with modified oil tanks and piping. The pattern of domination continued with Senna taking pole position on the grid n 1m 24.067s, with Prost second in 1m 24.134s. Mansell (normally aspirated Judd-powered Williams) was third fastest in 1m 24.269s with Boutsen (normally aspirated Benetton) fourth in 1m 24.904s. During qualifying neither McLaren driver was completely happy with his car, Prost was complaining of lack of grip and Senna, pushing hard, spun off on the Friday.

At the start Prost surged away into the lead, and he was to lead the race throughout, whilst Senna made a slightly slower start and at the end of the first lap he was back in third place behind Mansell's Williams. Throughout the race Senna received inaccurate and pessimistic forecasts from the on-board fuel computer, which restrained his performance and prevented him challenging for the lead. Prost won the race from Mansell and Nannini (Benetton) with Senna fourth and in fact Senna's McLaren ran out of fuel at the first corner after the finishing line. After this race Prost led the World Championship with 84 points (90 gross), whilst Senna had scored 79 points. The 1988 World Championship was still wide open.

Japanese Grand Prix

In the interval between Jerez and Suzuka, test driver Emanuele Pirro had extensively tested a new Honda engine set-up at the Japanese circuit. There were, however, few changes to the McLarens at this race, although all were now fitted with the new oil tank and modified piping, first seen on two of the cars at Jerez.

During the period between the two races Jean-Marie Balestre, President of FISA, had written to Honda requesting that every effort should be made

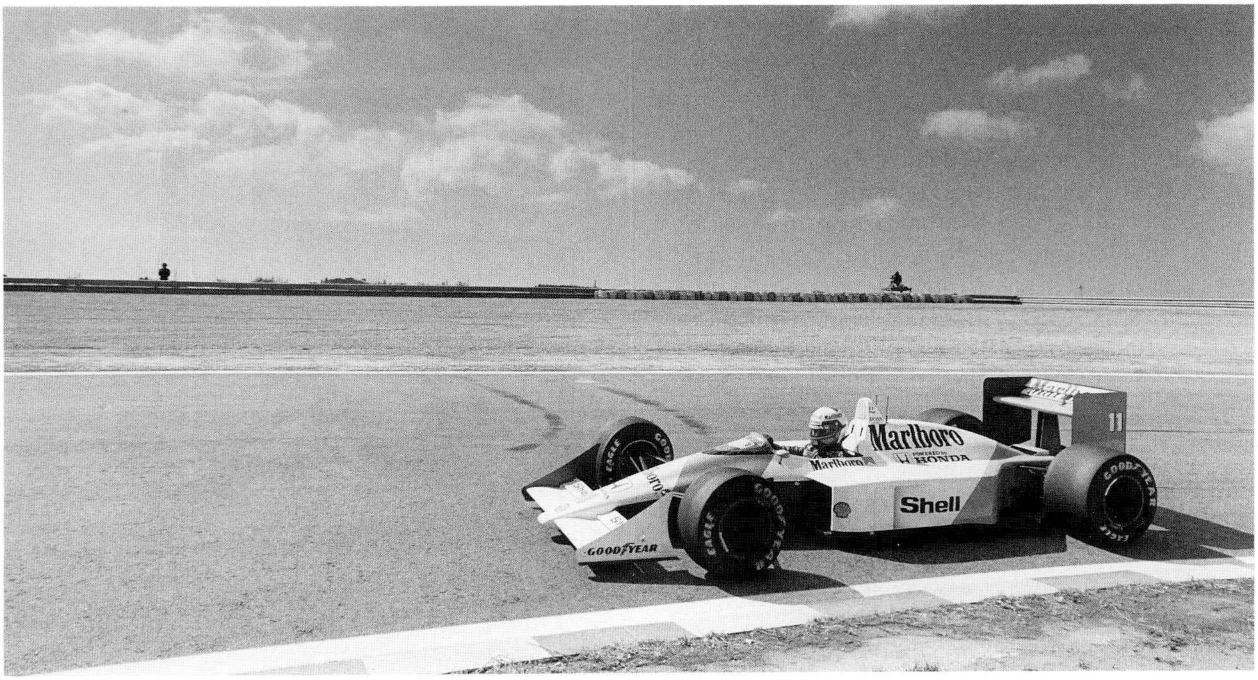

Alain Prost in the 1988 Portuguese Grand Prix at Estoril. He won the race from Senna and Capelli (March).

to ensure that the equipment supplied to the two McLaren drivers should be absolutely equal. Before Balestre's intervention, there had certainly been no suggestion that there was any inequality in equipment supplied to the two drivers, and Balestre in assessing the apparent disparity of performance between the two drivers over the preceding six or so Grands Prix, had ignored most of the factors that govern motor racing fortune. Honda were quite astounded by this letter, horrified at the suggestion that they should favour one driver against another and equally horrified at any suggestion that they should indulge in what amounted to a form of deception. Honda formally replied to FISA, publishing their reply, and this in turn prompted the publication of Balestre's letter. In the letter from Honda President, Tadashi Kume, he stated 'Honda Motor Co. Ltd sees fairness as the highest requirement of its philosophy for conducting business and sets its quality as an idealogy in its corporate dealings'. Later at a Honda press conference, the Honda spokesman said that so far as the company were concerned they were prepared to put the Honda engines in a line and let the drivers make their own choice. In writing this letter Balestre had created unnecessary controversy and it undoubtedly coloured relationships between McLaren and Honda on the one hand, and FISA on the other the following year.

During qualifying at Suzuka Senna was so pleased with the team's spare car, that he opted to keep this for the race and he took pole position in 1m 41.853s. It was Senna's spare car, set up for full-tank tests on the Saturday, that Prost was forced to abandon because of a fuel leak in the cockpit. The Frenchman took second place on the grid in 1m 42.177s, with Berger (Ferrari) third fastest and Capelli with the normally aspirated March in fourth place.

Prior to the Japanese race the World Championship ranking stood: Alain Prost 84 points (90 gross) and Ayrton Senna 79 points. If Senna won the Japanese race then he would have won the World Championship, for whatever points Prost scored at the final round at Adelaide would simply mean that he would have to drop other points scored during the year and could not match the Brazilian's total. Perhaps too determined to ensure that he gained victory, when the light turned green, Senna stalled his engine, let the clutch out and caught it, only to stall again. Because the grid at Suzuka was on a slope, he was able to roll forward and was fortunate enough to persuade the Honda engine to fire. At the end of the first lap Prost led from Berger, Capelli, Alboreto and Boutsen with Senna back in eighth place. By lap 4 Senna was in fourth place and Prost was now battling to hold off the second-place March of Capelli. At the end of lap 16 Capelli was a nose ahead as they crossed the start-finishing line. Prost regained the lead at the next corner. The March lasted only seven more laps before retiring with engine failure. On lap 11 Senna took third place from Berger, and after Capelli's retirement he steadily closed up on the leading McLaren. Prost's efforts to hold off the Brazilian were thwarted by a minor gearbox problem and Senna took the lead at the end of lap 27 when Prost missed a gear. Light rain began to fall five laps from the finish, and both Senna and Prost were forced to ease their pace with Senna gesticulating furiously and anxiously each time he passed the pits. At the chequered flag he was just over 13 seconds ahead of Prost, with Boutsen third, Berger fourth and Nannini with the second Benetton in fifth place. Senna had won his first World Championship.

Australian Grand Prix

During the Japanese event Balestre had been telephoning to Japan constantly asking that McLaren's progress should be carefully observed and after the race had requested that Prost's gearbox should be examined in detail by FISA. Ron Dennis bitterly resented this interference in the team's affairs and flatly refused to allow his cars to be submitted for scrutineering in the future on any other grounds than technical eligibility. He followed this up with a demand that Balestre and FISA should apologize for the suggestions that Senna had been favoured.

There were few changes to the McLarens at what was the last race of the turbocharged era. Honda had carefully tuned the engines so as to give maximum throttle response at Adelaide and although the team used the small turbochargers during Friday's qualifying, they changed to the larger turbochargers on the Saturday. Senna had slightly sprained his right wrist whilst playing football in Bali where he had been on holiday the preceding week. This wrist was to give him some trouble in both qualifying and the race, although he made light of the injury. Both drivers had minor complaints about the behaviour of their cars during qualifying but, inevitably, Senna took pole position in 1m 17.748s, with Prost second fastest in 1m 17.880s. Mansell (Williams) and Berger (Ferrari) were third and fourth fastest.

Prost was away first at the start, whilst Senna fumbled his start and Prost soon began to pull out a reasonable lead over his team-mate. As this was the last race of the formula and as Ferrari's prospects of success were virtually nil, Berger had made it very clear before the race that he was going to go flat out regardless of the state of his fuel. He moved up into second place on lap 3, banging wheels with Senna as he pushed his way past. Four laps later he passed Prost and he led the race until lap 26 when he collided with the Ligier of Arnoux which he was about to lap. As the race progressed it became obvious that Senna was struggling with gear-selection problems. Prost too was struggling with his gearbox and he also had to battle with an understeer problem when he lost one of the front wing skirts. With some 17 laps to go, Senna dropped 12 seconds as a result of second gear stripping completely and at Adelaide this was a major problem, because second gear was used in all five times on every lap. Over the radio Ron Dennis gave Senna clear instructions: use the highest possible boost settings and the richest fuel mixture on the fast parts of the course and ease back on the settings on the slower parts. Senna was able to continue to lap swiftly without second gear and to bring an end to the hopes of Piquet in third place with his Lotus from catching and challenging the second-place McLaren.

When Prost took the chequered flag at the end of the Adelaide, it was his 35th race victory,

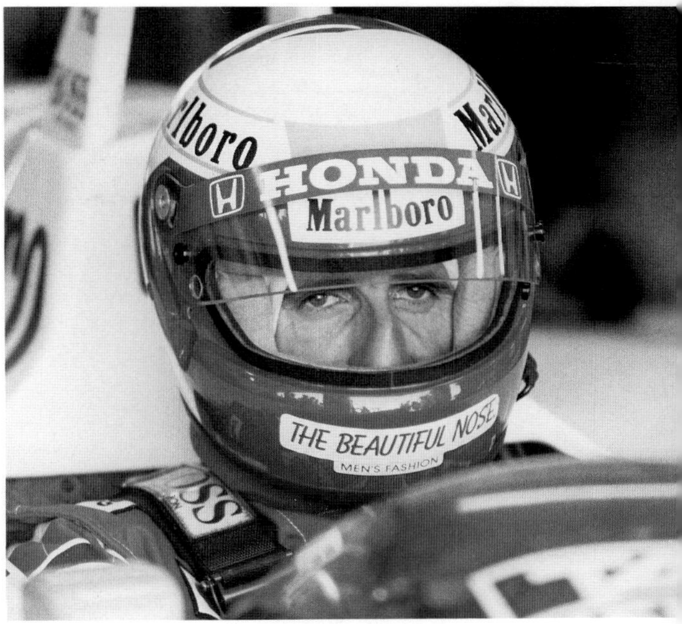

Alain Prost advertises 'The Beautiful Nose' at the 1988 Australian Grand Prix.

comfortably eight wins ahead of the previous record-holder Stewart (27). During the year McLaren had won 15 of the 16 races, eight victories to Senna and seven to Prost. The team had taken 15 pole positions, Senna 13 and Prost 2. Prost's score of Championship points (105 gross) was a record in itself although not good enough to win the Championship on the basis of the complicated calculations. McLaren's own total in the Constructors' Cup of 199 points was in itself a new and overwhelming record. It had been a year of complete satisfaction and fulfilment for McLaren's Ron Dennis, although Dennis still nursed one area of dissatisfaction. He had hoped so dearly that the team would win all the 16 races of the year, a possibility ruined when Senna tripped over Schlesser's Williams at Monza. For many enthusiasts however, the McLaren domination had brought an element of boredom into racing that had only been relieved by Berger's victory in the Italian race.

8: 1989: Conquest and Conflict

During the years 1987-88, when 3500 cc normally aspirated cars competed alongside the turbocharged cars, quite a number of new teams had entered the fray and some teams had made an early decision to switch to normally aspirated engines before they became compulsory for the 1990 season. In total 20 teams competed in Formula 1 during the 1989 season, but many of these were strugglers at the back of the field, either failing to pre-qualify or failing to qualify and, if they did qualify, trailing round well off the pace. Some of these teams had nowhere to go but down, including Osella, whose staying power at the back of the Formula 1 grids over the last few years had been remarkable, whilst others were newcomers well financed, with good prospects but a very substantial learning curve ahead of them.

The principle opposition to McLaren during 1989 was likely to come from Williams with their Renault V10-powered FW12C cars (this team had used Judd engines in 1989), March with the 881 cars (the Leyton House March Racing Team had impressed during the years 1987-88 and were regarded as being a very serious contender), the Ford-powered Benetton B188s and the new Ferrari Tipo 640 V12s designed by John Barnard.

Of these, Ferrari, Benetton and Williams were all to make their mark during the year, but March was to sadly disappoint, and the team's competitive edge was lost once it became independent from the March company. Occasionally also other drivers and other cars surprised by remarkable one-off performances.

For 1990 Neil Oatley developed the MP4/5, an evolutionary development of the first of the MP4 series and still retaining a carbon-fibre composite monocoque manufactured from material supplied by Hercules in the United States. The most significant changes to the McLaren were aerodynamic improvements that reflected the team's continuing aerodynamic research, but also met the requirements of the new V10 Honda engine for greater cooling. At the beginning of the season the cars raced with the David North-designed three-shaft longitudinal transmission, a development of that used in 1988, twin-caliper McLaren/Lockheed brakes, pull-rod suspension at the front and push-rod suspension at the rear. However, this was regarded as an interim stage in development and later McLaren would be producing a new transverse 6-speed gearbox, used with single-caliper Brembo brakes together with new rear suspension and front suspension uprights.

Led by project leader Osamu Goto, Honda had developed the RA109E 3490 cc (92 × 52.5 mm) V10 engine with the cylinders set at an angle of 72 degrees and gear drive for the twin overhead camshafts. The design of the McLaren had been well advanced when the Honda engineers suggested that gear drive should be adopted in place of the originally proposed belt drive, for although there would be additional weight and, partly because of the late stage at which it had been suggested, problems of installation, Honda were convinced that gear drive would provide far greater accuracy and control of valve timing. McLaren accepted Honda's recommendations without question. This Honda engine had first been shown to the public at the 1987 Tokyo Motor Show at which time its power output in bench testing was around 500 bhp, but following intensive development by Honda, and lengthy test sessions with modified MP4/4B chassis driven by Senna, Prost and the team's test driver Emanuele Pirro, by the start of 1989 the power output had reached 650 bhp. During the 1989 season power output rose to 685 bhp at 13,000 rpm. Power figures have always to be regarded with caution, but it would seem that the Honda's power output was a little higher than that of the Ferrari and the V10 Renault, but substantially greater than that of the Cosworth DFR (595 bhp), the Ford used by Benetton (something over 600 bhp), the Judd V8 (610 bhp) and the new Lamborghini V12.

Both Prost and Senna remained with the team, but their relationship, already not the best, rapidly deteriorated as the season progressed.

Brazilian Grand Prix

During the testing the week before, McLaren had only one car ready and the other two were flown out immediately before the Brazilian race. At this stage in the MP4/5's development there were only too obvious handling problems, with some degree of instability on high speed corners, and during qualifying at Rio de Janeiro neither driver was happy with his car. Nevertheless Senna took pole position in 1m 25.302s, with Patrese (Williams) alongside him on the grid in 1m 26.172s. Prost was back in fifth place in 1m 26.620s, slightly faster than Mansell (Ferrari) in 1m 26.772s.

Race day was incredibly hot, with the temperature at the circuit nudging 106 degrees Farenheit. At the start Senna was slow off the mark, Patrese went ahead with his Williams and Berger accelerated to the left of Senna. As the Ferrari and the McLaren entered the first right-hand corner, they banged wheels, Senna's McLaren lost its nose-cone and Berger's Ferrari spun to a halt. So the Williams-Renaults of Patrese and Boutsen led from Mansell, Prost and Capelli (March). Senna slowly made his way to the pits where a new nose-section was fitted. Berger also rejoined the race, but retired with internal engine problems on that first lap. On lap 3 Mansell passed a slowing Boutsen, the Williams driver coasted to a halt with a blown engine, and Prost was now in third place. When Prost made his first stop for tyres at the end of lap 14 the order became Patrese, Mansell, Capelli and Warwick (Arrows). Senna was still struggling round in last place, but rapidly making up ground. Prost, however, had a problem unknown to other competitors. Shortly after his pit stop for tyres, his clutch had begun to fail and whilst he could drive making clutchless gear changes, there was no possibility of a further stop for tyres. Mansell now led the race, except for two laps, laps 45 and 46, when the Ferrari driver stopped for a further tyre change and at the same time had a loose steering wheel replaced. At the end of this 61-lap race Mansell won by around eight seconds from Prost, with Gugelmin (March) third, Herbert (Benetton) a brilliant fourth on his Grand Prix début, Warwick (Arrows) fifth and Nannini (Benetton) sixth. Senna finished in 11th place, two laps in arrears.

San Marino Grand Prix

There were no substantial changes to the McLarens at the Imola circuit, but the team's continuing development work made itself only too obvious in practice, with Senna taking pole position in 1m 26.010s, Prost second fastest in 1m 26.235s and Mansell (Ferrari) third in 1m 27.652s.

The Imola race made its impact on world headlines, not because the McLarens had reasserted their supremacy with Senna and Prost taking first and second places, a lap ahead of third-place man Nannini (Bennetton); nor was it the apparent further breakdown in relations between Senna and Prost that

Alain Prost with the new V10 Honda-powered MP4/5 at the first race of the 1989 season, the Brazilian Grand Prix. The race was won by Nigel Mansell (Ferrari) and Prost finished second.

came out into the open after the race. The event that dominated the news from Imola was Gerhard Berger's miraculous escape from his Ferrari which went off the road at the flat-out Tamburello left-hand corner, hit the concrete walls, skidded round and skated along the barrier for nearly 200 yards. No sooner had it come to rest than the Ferrari exploded in flames. Thanks mainly to the extremely prompt reaction of the fire marshalls, Berger was rescued from the burning Ferrari, suffering only a broken rib, a lineal fracture of the left shoulder blade, second degree burns on the hands and chemical burns. He remained in hospital only until that evening, was flown by private jet to Innsbruck for treatment, reappeared at Monaco shortly afterwards (not to race, but he missed only that one event in the year) and seemed totally unscathed mentally by this horrific accident.

Following Berger's crash, the race was stopped, with three laps completed, restarted as a second part of 55 laps with the results on the aggregate of the two parts. When the race was restarted, Prost was away first, but Senna snatched the inside line into Tosa corner and by the end of the lap had pulled out a lead of more than a second. This was the order until the finish. There had been a clear understanding between Prost and Senna that whoever led into the first corner would not be passed by his team-mate and Prost believed that Senna whom he regarded as being 'not the man of honour' had breached this agreement.

Although Senna subsequently, rather grudgingly, apologised to Prost, from this point on the two drivers barely spoke to each other and all essential communications with regard to technical matters relating to the cars took place between their engineers Steve Nichols and Neil Oatley.

Monaco Grand Prix

Although the team was still using the longitudinal three-shaft gearbox, some changes were seen on the McLarens, including the new single caliper brakes which had originally been intended for use with the new gearbox, new front and rear suspension uprights and a saving of weight, partly in the chassis and partly by a weight reduction in the Honda engine. Senna was sensationally fast in practice, taking pole position in 1m 22.308s, whilst Prost was second fastest in 1m 23.456s. Prost's qualifying had been far from troublefree, for on the Friday he had stripped second gear and, after switching to the spare, flat-spotted the tyres by an excursion up the St. Devote escape road. He was far from happy with the spare car because of a vibration problem. Third and fourth in qualifying were Boutsen (Williams) and Brundle (Brabham).

Despite gearbox problems towards the end of the race, Senna turned in an immaculate performance at Monaco, leading throughout whilst Prost later admitted that he had given up his pursuit of Senna, after being baulked by Arnoux (Ligier) and being forced to brake to a stop after a collision between Nelson Piquet (Lotus) and fourth-place driver de Cesaris (Dallara) had blocked the track. Prost's frank admission shocked his enthusiasts and supporters considerably and it looked as though he had lost his will to win. In third place at the finish was young Stefano Modena (Brabham), a lap in arrears, and fourth Caffi (Dallara).

Mexican Grand Prix

There were no changes to the McLarens other than that the Honda engines had been specially modified to suit the high altitude of the Hermanos Rodriguez circuit. Because it was becoming only too apparent that McLaren's 1988 domination was reasserting itself, there were numerous rumours and proposals as to how to make racing more interesting and keep the attention of television viewers worldwide. One suggestion was that there should be compulsory pit stops and this was regarded as being quite a serious proposition, promoted as it was by Bernie Ecclestone. Happily no such developments took place during 1989. Senna and Prost again took the first two positions on the grid, with times of 1m 17.876s and 1m 18.773s. With this pole qualifying position, Senna had equalled Jim Clark's record of 33 pole positions, although by the end of the season Senna had extended that record to 42. Behind the McLaren drivers came Mansell (1m 19.137s), and Capelli (1m 19.337s), whilst Berger on his return to racing was sixth fastest in 1m 19.835s.

At the start Senna took the lead, Mansell accelerated through into second place ahead of Prost. Modena lost control of his Brabham at the Peralta curve and hit the Ligier of Grouillard, Caffi spun his Dallara and Capelli veered off into the run-off area. Out came the red flag to stop the race. The race was restarted with the original grid positions, but the distance reduced by one lap. Once again Mansell accelerated hard, trying to find a gap between Senna and Prost, but the McLarens accelerated into the lead with Berger coming through to take third place from Mansell. During the opening laps Prost chased Senna hard, but had to stop for a change of tyres at the end of lap 20. It was a slow stop and although over the radio Prost had asked for 'Bs' all round, the same set-up as Senna had fitted, by mistake the McLaren team fitted 'Cs' all round again. It was all purely a mistake, and a very unhappy Prost rushed back into the field in sixth place and Senna was now unchallenged. For soon Prost's left rear tyre began to blister, another stop was necessary and once again the McLaren team messed up the tyre change, fitting 'Bs' on the left only and making another slow change. At the finish Senna was over 15 seconds ahead of Patrese (Williams) with Alboreto (Tyrrell) third, Nannini (Benetton) and Prost, in fifth place. Senna now led the World Championship with 27 points to the 20 of Prost.

United States Grand Prix

Once again there was just the single race in the United States, but now held at Phoenix in Arizona, over yet another boring street circuit of 2.36 miles with slow lap times, a succession of 90-degree corners and lined by concrete barriers topped by catch-fencing. For this race Honda had made further modifications to the RA109E engines, specifically to cope with the very high temperatures expected at this circuit. Oil coolers suspended under the rear aerofoils were regarded as an infringement of the regulations, so far as drivers' rear vision was concerned, and Senna's times with the spare during the first qualifying session were disallowed. This mattered little to Senna whose subsequent times were searingly fast and he dominated practice with pole in 1m 30.108s, his 34th pole position, and now Clark's record had not just been matched but exceeded. For Prost, not all went well during qualifying, for on the Friday he had gear selection problems and he crashed during the morning untimed session on Saturday, badly damaging the monocoque. With the spare car he took second place on the grid in 1m 31.517s, ahead of Nannini (Benetton) and Mansell (Ferrari).

Initially the race followed the inevitable pattern. Prost edged away first at the start, but as they went into the first corner, Prost on the right of the track hit a bad bump, wheel-spin caused the engine to hit the rev limiter, the engine stopped momentarily, and Senna was able to pass on the left. Behind the McLarens came Nannini, Mansell, Caffi (Dallara) and Modena (Brabham). McLaren domination was halved on lap 28 as Senna passed the pits with an engine misfire which worsened and at the end of lap 34 he pulled into the pits, allowing Prost to take the lead. The McLaren mechanics changed the engine management control box and the battery and although Senna resumed the race in 15th place, he retired 12 laps later with the same problem. Prost was now unchallenged and was able to lap with comfortable ease and at the end of this 75-lap race led across the line from Patrese (Williams), Cheever (Arrows), Danner (Rial), Herbert (Benetton) and Boutsen (Williams). But the fourth, fifth and sixth place finishers were all a lap in arrears. Prost had now snatched the advantage in the World Championship with 29 points to the 27 of Senna.

Canadian Grand Prix

The results at the Gilles Villeneuve circuit were to prove the first upset of the season. For the first time since the 1988 Portuguese Grand Prix, Senna was bested during qualifying and Prost took pole position in 1m 20.973s, with Senna second fastest in 1m 21.049s, and Patrese (Williams) and Berger (Ferrari) third and fourth.

Race day proved cold and cloudy, and throughout the race there was rain, heavy at times, and it was officially declared a Wet Race. Berger stalled on the grid, so there had to be a fresh line-up. After the parade lap both Mansell and Nannini decided to change tyres, which meant starting from the pit lane. Both motored to the end of the pit lane, expecting to find an official blocking off the access to the track. There was no one there, both assumed the race had already started and rushed out on to the circuit. The field was still on the grid, and as a result, mainly because of the incompetence of the officials in Canada rather than any error of the drivers, both Mansell and Nannini were disqualified for a breach of the regulations. Prost had led away from the start from Senna, but at the end of the lap Prost was convinced that he had a puncture. A stop at the pits revealed nothing wrong and he rejoined the race only to have the top left front suspension pick-up point pull out of the monocoque.

Senna continued in the lead until the end of lap 4 when he stopped at the pit to fit slicks, hoping to benefit from improving weather conditions, and he rejoined the race in fifth place. The race leaders were now Patrese and Boutsen, ahead of Senna who was closing rapidly, Warwick (Arrows) and Arnoux (Ligier). As the intensity of the rain varied, so the drivers made different decisions as to what tyres they should be fitted. Senna had closed on Boutsen, but in heavier rain he dropped back rapidly so that by the end of lap 20 he was 26 seconds in arrears and he stopped again for wet tyres. Now Patrese led the field, whilst Boutsen who had stopped twice, first for slicks and then for wet weather tyres, had dropped well down the field. When Patrese stopped for new wet tyres at the end of lap 35, Warwick took the lead with his Arrows, but within four laps Senna was back in front. Senna resumed the lead on lap 39 ahead of Patrese and Boutsen, but on Patrese's Williams two bolts had fallen out from the rear undertray, taking away much of the downforce, so that Boutsen caught and passed his Italian team-mate. Four laps later Senna's Honda engine failed because of electronic problems and the Belgian Williams driver found himself back in the lead. At the finish Boutsen led Patrese across the line by a margin of a little over 30 seconds with de Cesaris's Dallara third, Piquet's Lotus fourth and Arnoux' Ligier in fifth place, a lap in arrears. It had been a shambles of a race because of the weather conditions but the result was one that was to do much to buck up interest in the season's racing.

French Grand Prix

At the Paul Ricard circuit a number of changes could be seen on the McLarens. There was a new car for Prost, MP4/5-5 which had a stiffened front monocoque (the existing chassis were also strengthened at this point) and there were a number of other minor changes. Practice was relatively troublefree, and Prost took pole position in 1m 07.203s, with Senna second fastest in 1m 07.228s, Mansell third in 1m 07.455s and Nannini fourth in 1m 08.137s. Despite the continuing threat from Ferrari, and the increasing strength of the Benetton and Williams teams, the race proved another McLaren benefit and Prost led the race almost throughout. He did not lead at the start, because Senna made a superb getaway and gained a small advantage ahead of his French team-mate; after Gugelmin's March collided with Boutsen and crashed on to the track upside down the race was restarted. At the restart Senna again led away, but suddenly slowed because a spur gear in the differential had broken, and Prost took a lead which he retained throughout this 80-lap race. After starting from the pit lane, Mansell came through to finish second, with Patrese third, Alesi (Tyrrell) fourth, Johansson (Onyx) fifth, Grouillard (Ligier) sixth, the last two both a lap in arrears. Prost now led the World Championship with 38 points to the 27 of Senna and in the Constructors' Cup McLaren had amassed a grand total of 65 points, compared with the 35 of Williams in second place.

British Grand Prix

At long last the McLaren team appeared with the new transverse 6-speed gearbox after long and extensive testing. However, there had been a manufacturing fault which resulted in problems with the oil system and destroyed McLaren's prospects of fast lap times during practice on the Friday. Although Neil Oatley returned to the factory at Woking to draw modifications to the oil system, these resulted in no solution to the problem and on the Saturday, just as on the Friday, the cars were laying a smoke haze. One of the major problems was that the engine oil tank was built into the transmission casing. Despite all these problems Senna took pole in 1m 09.099s, with Prost second in 1m 09.266s, and with the Ferraris of Mansell and Berger in third and fourth places. On the Saturday the McLaren technicians had been trying to locate the problem and believed that they had traced it to faulty welds within the oil tanks. By the start of the race the necessary changes had been made to the cars.

Almost inevitably Senna took the lead, followed by Prost and Mansell. Behind the Brazilian Prost kept a watching brief, only too well aware that there was a problem with Senna's car and as Prost commented later, 'two or three times he nearly spun'. At Becketts on lap 12 Senna lost control, the McLaren spun viciously and Senna shot off into the gravel backwards. Prost now led from Mansell, with the French driver struggling to hold off Mansell's attack, but as the race continued Prost gradually built up a lead of a little over eight seconds. A puncture and a pit stop for new tyres destroyed any prospects of Mansell challenging for the lead. Prost made a precautionary stop for new tyres at the end of lap 47, anxious about vibrations that were clearly caused by

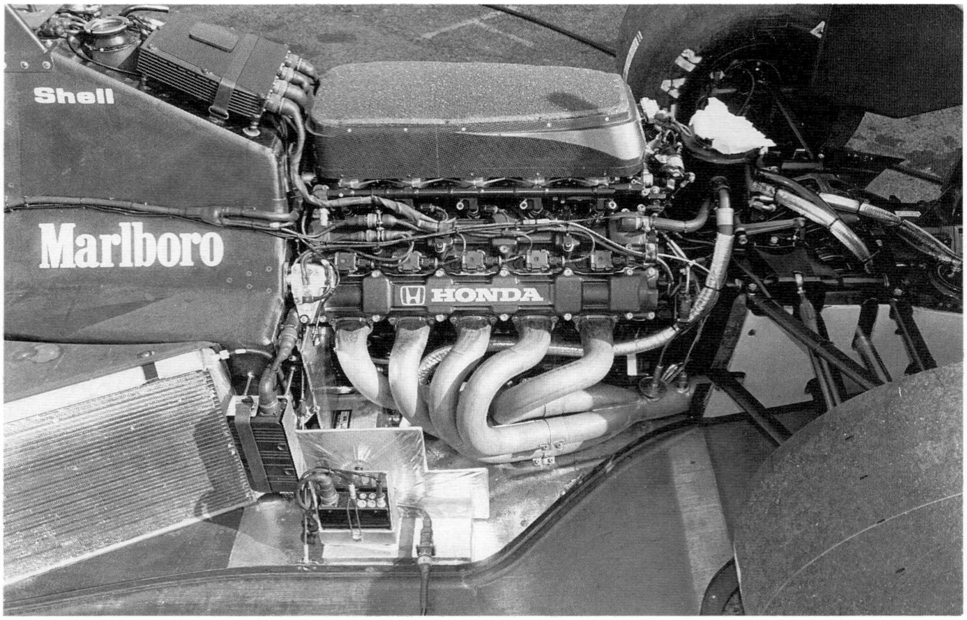

The V10 Honda RA109E engine seen installed in the MP4/5 chassis at the 1989 French Grand Prix.

In the French Grand Prix Alain Prost scored his second win of the year, while Ayrton Senna retired because of differential failure.

worn rubber, and despite a 25-second stop because of a problem with the right-rear wheel, Prost was able to rejoin the race 12 seconds ahead of Mansell. At the finish Prost led by over 19 seconds from Mansell with Nannini (Benetton) third, Piquet (Lotus) fourth, Martini (Minardi) and Sala (Minardi) fifth and sixth, a lap in arrears. Prost now led the World Championship with 47 points to the 27 of Senna.

German Grand Prix

At Hockenheim all the McLarens were fitted with the new transverse gearbox and the problems seemed to have been cured. Senna took pole position in 1m 42.300s, but his qualifying was far from troublefree. During Friday morning's untimed session Senna lost control, spun across the grass and shunted the barriers backwards. Towards the end of the first qualifying session he ran over a large stone dislodged at the last corner by another competitor, which punched a hole in the monocoque. However, the McLaren test team had stayed in France a day at Dijon on their way to the following week's tests at Imola and so their transporter was diverted to Hockenheim. The rear end of the test car was linked to Senna's damaged car. Despite gearbox problems, Prost was second fastest in 1m 43.295s, followed on the grid by Mansell and Berger.

Berger was first away at the start, but he was passed swiftly by both Senna and Prost on that first lap, and the McLarens again dominated the race. Senna led Prost until lap 18 when Prost stopped for new tyres, was delayed because the clutch was not disengaging fully, and he had to keep the car in neutral while the wheel nuts were done up. He rejoined the race in fourth place, but assumed the lead when Senna made his pit stop at the end of lap 20. Senna battled to get to grips with Prost, on lap 43 Prost suddenly slowed when sixth gear would not engage and the Brazilian took the lead. He won the race by 18 seconds from Prost, with Mansell a consistent third and Patrese with his Williams in fourth place, a lap in arrears. Prost still comfortably led the World Championship with 53 points to the 36 of Senna.

Hungarian Grand Prix

The Hungarian race was notable for the fact that for the first time after 17 races McLaren was not in pole position and a storming victory by Mansell did much to reawaken the world's flagging interest in Grand Prix racing. Ricardo Patrese took pole position on the grid in his Williams in 1m 19.726s, with Senna second fastest in 1m 20.039s. Remarkably, third place went to Alex Caffi with his Dallara in 1m 20.704s. Boutsen (Williams) was fourth fastest in 1m 21.001s and Prost was fifth with a time of 1m 21.076s.

It was a very similar story in the race. Patrese made a brilliant start, cutting across Senna and leading from Senna, Caffi, Berger and Prost. Patrese maintained his lead until the end of lap 52 by when the water temperature on the Williams was dangerously high. Senna slipped into the lead and Mansell followed through into second place. After only another two laps Patrese retired with a holed water radiator. Time and time again Mansell tried to pass the leading McLaren, but it was not until lap 58 when his chance came, when Johansson having just rejoined the race with his Onyx and slowed by gear selection trouble, forced Senna momentarily to back off, whilst Mansell pulled to the right; the Ferrari and the McLaren almost collided, but Mansell kept his foot down and led into the next corner. By the end of this 77-lap race Mansell had pulled out a lead over Senna of over 25 seconds, Boutsen took third place and Prost was fourth.

Belgian Grand Prix

Normality returned at Spa Francorchamps, where Senna took pole position in 1m 50.867s, with Prost second fastest in 1m 51.463s. Behind the McLarens the order was Berger – Boutsen – Patrese – Mansell. The race was run in wet, cold conditions and the two McLarens led throughout, Senna crossing the line ahead of Prost who had struggled for much of the race to hold off Mansell's Ferrari which finished third ahead of Boutsen.

Ayrton Senna in the German Grand Prix which he won from Prost.

Italian Grand Prix

Although speculation had been rife for weeks, it was only on the Thursday before the Italian Grand Prix that it was announced that Alain Prost would be joining Ferrari in 1990. The McLaren team appeared to have taken Prost's defection in good part, but relations within the team worsened over the weekend of the Italian race. Senna in sparkling form took pole in 1m 23.72s, with the Ferraris of Berger and Mansell second and third fastest and Prost fourth in 1m 25.510s.

Inevitably, Senna led away and at the end of the first lap he appeared to be pulling away from Berger, Mansell and Prost. Not only was Senna at the peak of his form, but the McLaren was more powerful and handling better than the Ferrari opposition. Prost took third place on lap 21 and moved up into second place behind his team-mate on lap 41. When Mansell slowed on lap 42, because of engine problems, the Williams FW12Cs of Boutsen and Patrese streamed through into fourth and fifth places. On lap 42, only 10 laps from the finish, Senna's engine blew up spectacularly on the approach to the Parabolica and he spun off on his own oil. So Prost finished the race the winner a little over 13 seconds ahead of Berger, Boutsen and Patrese. The prize-giving was marred by the ill-feeling within the McLaren team. As Prost stood holding the winner's trophies, acting with some inexplicable impulse Prose

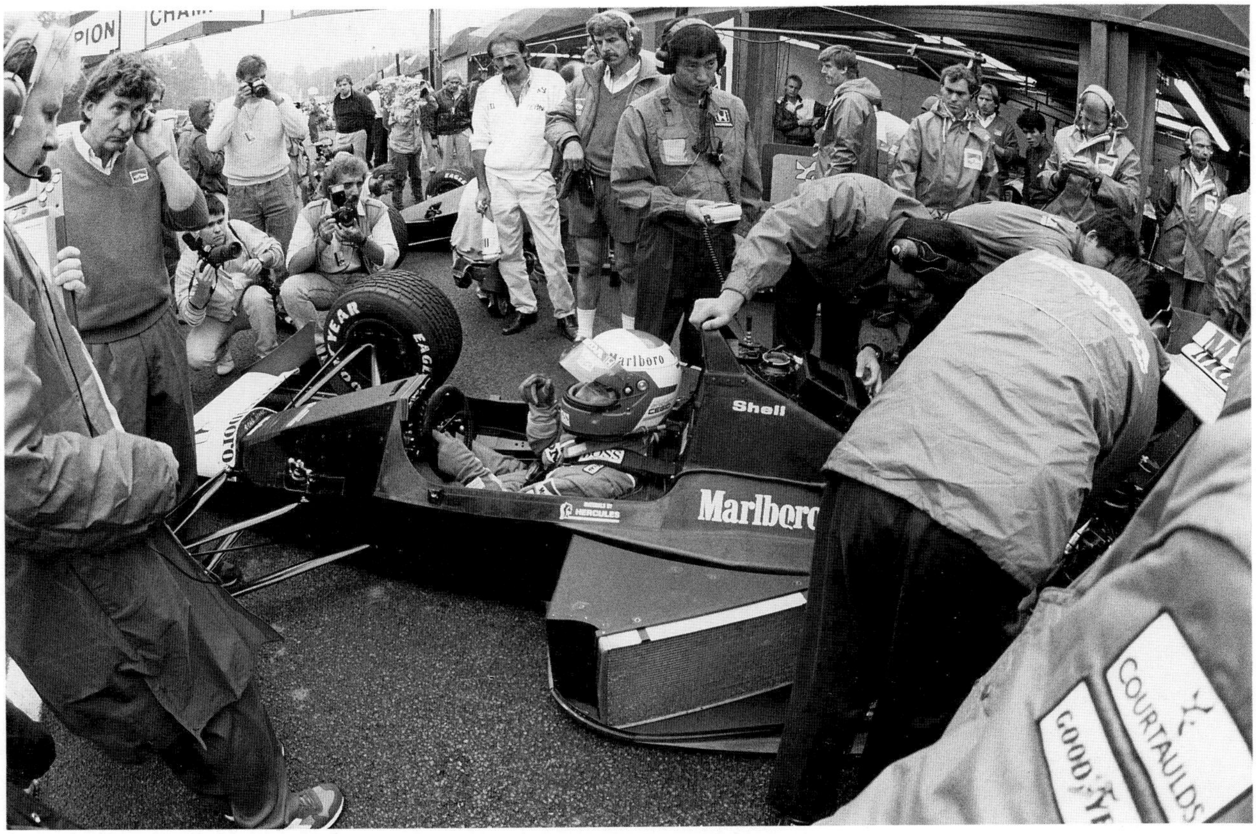

Alain Prost and the MP4/5 in the pits at the 1989 Belgian Grand Prix.

handed one of the trophies to the Ferrari supporters. Enraged, Ron Dennis threw another trophy at Prost's feet and walked off. At the Press briefing afterwards, Prost expanded at length on his unhappiness in the McLaren team and the bad treatment that he thought that he was receiving from Honda.

Portuguese Grand Prix

At the start of the weekend at Estoril Marlboro McLaren McLaren issued a statement signed by Ron Dennis, Yoshinobu Noguchi (PR Manager of Honda) and Prost which said amongst other things '. . . Alain Prost, Honda and McLaren have had extensive discussions and wish, via this joint statement, to put on record their intentions for creating the best possible working environment for the driver and the team for the remainder of the season. Honda and McLaren have again reassured Alain, to his satisfaction, of their commitment to equality and will continue this policy regardless of Alain's move to another team for the 1990 season.

'Alain deeply regrets the adverse publicity and the resulting embarrassment that had been caused by his actions. . .

'The team also expressed its disdain and dissatisfaction over inacurate, unqualified and damaging statements made by third parties subsequent to Monza . . .' It was all a rather futile attempt to paper over the cracks and the remarks in the third paragraph were aimed at suggestions by FISA over uneven treatment of the two drivers by Honda, but it was open to misunderstanding and quite a number of people thought that the words were addressed to other drivers who had experience of Honda in the past at Williams and had been expounding their views of the situation. In any event Prost may have signed the statement, but this did nothing to stop him to continue privately complaining about Honda and the team.

At Estoril Senna took pole in 1m 15.468s, ahead of the Ferraris of Berger and Mansell, with Prost fourth fastest in 1m 16.204s. On this circuit at least, the Ferraris were a match for the McLarens; Berger led on the first lap from Senna, Mansell and Prost and on lap 8 Mansell moved up into second place behind his Austrian team-mate. On lap 24 Mansell took the lead from Berger, whose tyres had now gone off and who had been baulked by back markers. During the routine tyre changes Martini's Minardi fleetingly led the race. Mansell's tyre stop was one of the most controversial events in a controversial year. When he pulled into the pits, he overshot the Ferrari pit, but instead of waiting to be pushed back he selected reverse. From that moment on Mansell's race was in effect over and he was shortly to be disqualified.

By lap 43, Berger was back in the lead with Mansell second on the road and Senna third. Both Mansell and Senna claimed that they could not see the black flag displayed at the start-finish line because they were passing the pits at around 170 mph and driving into the sun. In the McLaren pit there was more than some degree of anxiety and on the radio link Ron Dennis urged Senna to ignore Mansell. Senna failed to hear the message clearly, asked Dennis to repeat it, but it was all too late. Mansell pulled out from behind Senna, drew alongside the McLaren and took the line into the corner. Senna held firm, would not give way, and the McLaren's right-rear wheel hit the left-front wheel of the Ferrari, and both drivers spun into the gravel on the outside of the circuit. Mansell stalked back to the pits without even looking at Senna, whilst Senna stood, dazed, contemplating the loss of valuable World Championship points. Subsequently Mansell was called before the Stewards, to whom he apologized and explained that he had not seen the black flag. As a result he and Ferrari were fined $50,000 and he was subsequently banned from the next race, the Spanish Grand Prix. Berger won the race from Prost and the Onyx of Johansson.

Spanish Grand Prix

If Senna was to win the World Championship, he had to win two of the last three races of the season. Qualifying at Jerez started badly for the team, for during the first qualifying session on the Friday afternoon Senna raced past black flags, waved yellow flags at the scene of the serious accident where Foitek had crashed badly with his Rial after the rear wing had collapsed and then past the red flag at the start-finish line. For this Senna was fined $20,000 and his times up to that point were disregarded. Even so, Senna still reigned supreme in qualifying and took pole position in 1m 20.291s, with Berger second fastest in 1m 20.565s, Prost third in 1m 21.368s and Martini (Minardi) a surprising and brilliant fourth.

Senna led every lap and won the race at 106.486 mph, a victory apparently made so much easier for him by the absence of Mansell's Ferrari worrying at his exhausts. Berger with the solitary Ferrari took second place, with Prost third and Alesi (Tyrrell) in fourth place, a lap in arrears.

Japanese Grand Prix

At Suzuka there was a new chassis, No.8 for Prost and all four cars at the circuit featured revised front suspension geometry. The McLarens were at peak form with Senna taking pole position in 1m 38.041s, Prost second fastest in 1m 39.771s and the Ferraris of Berger and Mansell on the second row of the grid. Most of the other teams were angered by the fact that McLaren had conducted three days' testing at Suzuka, breaching an agreement that teams would not test at a circuit immediately prior to a Grand Prix. McLaren's explanation was that when they had signed this agreement it was on the basis that their Japan-based testing team was not covered by the agreement and indeed they had correspondence from FOCA which supported them. And in any event, said Ron Dennis, it had rained during the test and there had also been other problems.

Because of the gradient of the road at the start, there was a shorter interval than usual at the start between the red and green lights. When the green light showed Prost was ready, whilst Senna was slow away and by the end of the first lap Prost led from Senna by over a second, gradually extending his lead. In third and fourth places were Berger and Nannini (Benetton). After the first round of tyre changes, Senna attacked Prost fiercely, despite being baulked by Piquet's Lotus, breaking the lap record and closing right on his team-mate. At the chicane on lap 46 Senna had a go at passing, forcing his McLaren alongside Prost and intimidating the Frenchman into backing off; on this so important day, Prost would not give way, the two McLarens collided and came to a halt in the middle of the track. Whilst Prost stepped out of his car immediately, Senna demanded and received an illegal push-start, and when the engine fired he drove out the exit of the escape road, by-passing the chicane.

Nannini (Benetton) now led the field, but Senna, even more determined than ever, tore into the pits for a new nose-cone to be fitted and rejoined the race 4.6 seconds behind the leader. It was at the approach to the chicane that Senna caught Nannini, forcing his way through while Nannini had the good sense to back off and let the Brazilian take the lead which he retained for the last two laps before the chequered flag. After a delay at the finish, Senna was disqualified (McLaren lodged an appeal immediately) and Nannini was declared the race winner, ahead of Patrese and Boutsen (Williams-Renaults). Prost had won the World Championship, provided that his own team-mate's appeal did not succeed and if Senna's appeal did not succeed, then the outcome of the final race of the year at Adelaide was irrelevent to the results of the World Championship. At the present time the appeal has not been finally settled, although it does seem unlikely that it will be allowed.

Australian Grand Prix

At Adelaide McLaren's dominant year was to end on a low note. During the dry qualifying sessions Senna took pole in 1m 16.665s, Prost was second in 1m 17.403s, Martini with the Minardi third fastest and Nannini in fourth place.

Race day dawned dry and cool, but by the start of the race torrential rain was falling. Relentless pressure was put on the drivers to accept that the totally impossible weather conditions were safe for racing by both FISA officials and by local officials. The Clerk of the Course, Tim Schenken, himself a former Formula 1 driver, was under immense pressure politically and sanctioned the running of the race against what must have been his better judgment. After arguments and discussion the parade lap started. Prost alone had the guts to complete the parade lap and pull into the pits, but nobody followed his example. With Prost missing from his place on the grid, Nannini was able to accelerate into the lead with Martini in second place, but without any real visibility Senna had managed to come through to the front by the end of lap 5, ahead of Boutsen, Patrese and Nannini. A mere nine laps later Senna who had already spun, ran straight into the back of the Brabham of Martin Brundle. Senna later admitted quite frankly that the conditions were so bad that he did not see the Brabham until after he felt the impact. In these appalling conditions the eventual winner was Boutsen (Williams) from Nannini (Benetton), Patrese (Williams) and Nakajima (Lotus) with Pirro (Benetton), fifth two laps in arrears and Martini sixth, three laps in arrears.

That the race should never have been run is beyond doubt or argument and it was a dismal end to a long controversial season of discontent. Prost took the World Championship with 76 points (81 gross) with Senna's total, excluding the Japanese race, 60 points and McLaren won the Constructors' Cup with 141 points to the 77 of Williams.

9: 1990: Introduction to the year

For 1990 McLaren developed the MP4/5B, a logical development of the 1989 car, incorporating significant aerodynamic changes, modified gearbox and suspension geometry, taller (because of changes in the safety regulations concerning cockpit size) and with a room for increased fuel capacity. Whilst Honda had a V12 engine under development, McLaren continued to use the familiar V10 engine raced in 1989, but with a number of modifications.

There had been a number of changes in the team. Steve Nichols had left to join Ferrari. Gerhard Berger had now joined Senna in the McLaren team, whilst Jonathan Palmer had become the team's official test driver.

The new car appeared in testing at Silverstone, but was crashed by Senna at Bridge Bend, when he spun over the kerbing and damaged the monocoque and undertray.

Throughout the winter months there had been disputes between FISA and McLaren and there were doubts whether Senna would be granted the necessary Superlicence for him to drive in Formula 1. FISA had threatened that Senna would not be permitted in Formula 1, unless he apologised for his behaviour in the latter part of 1989. Eventually, after a great deal of under the counter negotiations, a deal was struck between McLaren and FISA and Senna was granted his Superlicence.

United States Grand Prix

The first of the 1990 races was the United States event held at Phoenix in Arizona. Despite minor problems during qualifying, Berger took pole position in 1m 28.664s with Pierluigi Martini a surprising second on the grid with his Minardi. Senna was back in fifth place with a time of 1m 29.431s after problems during qualifying, including electrical trouble on the Friday, and because of rain on Saturday he had no chance of improving his time. He took third place at the first corner, chased hard after Berger, moving up into second place when the Austrian spun on lap 9, and then rapidly closed on the race-leader Alesi. Alesi fought hard to hold off the Brazilian, but Senna went ahead to win his 21st Grand Prix by a margin of close to 9 seconds from the Tyrrell driver. Boutsen (Williams) and Piquet (Benetton) finished third and fourth. After his spin into a tyre barrier, Berger had made his way back to the pits, rejoining with new tyres and a new rear wing, but retired with clutch failure after setting fastest lap.

Brazilian Grand Prix

The Brazilian race was held on the new Interlagos circuit, at a time when Brazil was in an even

In the Brazilian Grand Prix Gerhard Berger finished second.

greater state of financial chaos than usual. Senna took pole position in 1m 17.277s with Berger second fastest in 1m 17.888s. Initially Senna and Berger held first two places in the race, but they were split by Boutsen who moved up into second place with his Williams on lap 8. Senna lost his lead briefly when he stopped for new tyres, but then went ahead again until he collided with Nakajima (Tyrrell, losing the nose cone, dropping back to finish third, whilst Berger eventually took second place, slowed by a painful right foot that made braking difficult. The race was won by Prost (Ferrari).

With only two races of the season run, it was clear that McLaren still remained a strong force in racing, albeit now challenged by the much improved Ferrari opposition and with other teams well to the fore.

Appendix 1

McLaren Racing Performances with TAG and Honda-powered cars, 1983-89

1983

Dutch Grand Prix, Zandvoort,
28 August, 190.228 miles
Retired, N. Lauda (MP4/1E-6), brakes

Italian Grand Prix, Monza,
11 September, 187.403 miles
Retired, J. Watson (MP4/1E-5), engine
Retired, N. Lauda (MP4/1E-6), electrics

European Grand Prix, Brands Hatch,
25 September, 198.63 miles
Retired, J. Watson (MP4/1E-5), rear wing failure
Retired, N. Lauda (MP4/1E-6), engine

South African Grand Prix, Kyalami,
15 October, 196.35 miles
Disqualified, J. Watson (MP4/1E-7)
11th, N. Lauda (MP4/1E-6), not running at the finish, electrics

Drivers' World Championship:
6th, J. Watson, 22 points
10th, N. Lauda, 12 points

Constructors' Cup:
5th, McLaren, 34 points

1984

Brazilian Grand Prix, Rio de Janeiro,
25 March, 190.692 miles
1st, A. Prost (MP4/2-2), 1h 42m 34.492s (111.543 mph)
Retired, N. Lauda (MP4/2-1), electrics

South African Grand Prix, Kyalami,
7 April, 191.247 miles
1st, N. Lauda (MP4/2-1), 1h 29m 23.430s (128.367 mph)
2nd, A. Prost (MP4/2-3)

Belgian Grand Prix, Zolder, 29 April,
185.38 miles
Retired, A. Prost (MP4/2-2), distributor
Retired, N. Lauda (MP4/2-1), water pump

San Marino Grand Prix, Imola, 6 May,
187.90 miles
1st, A. Prost (MP4/2-3), 1hr 36m 53.679s (116.354 mph)
Retired, N. Lauda (MP4/2-1), piston failure

French Grand Prix, Dijon-Prenois,
20 May, 186.535 miles
1st, N. Lauda (MP4/2-1), 1h 31m 11.951s, 125.531 mph
7th, A. Prost (MP4/2-2), 1 lap in arrears

Monaco Grand Prix, Monte Carlo,
3 June, 63.797 miles (race stopped short)
1st, A. Prost (MP4/2-2), 1h 1m 07.740s, 62.619 mph
Retired, N. Lauda (MP4/2-1), spun off

Canadian Grand Prix, Circuit Gilles Villeneuve, Montreal, 17 June,
191.82 miles
2nd, N. Lauda (MP4/2-1)
3rd, A. Prost (MP4/2-2)

United States Grand Prix (Detroit),
Detroit, 24 June, 157.500 miles
5th, A. Prost (MP4/2-2)
Retired, N. Lauda (MP4/2-1), electrics

United States Grand Prix (Dallas), Dallas,
8 July, 162.408 miles
Retired, N. Lauda (MP4/2-1), hit wall
Retired, A. Prost (MP4/2-2), hit wall

British Grand Prix, Brands Hatch,
22 July, 185.566 miles
1st, N. Lauda (MP4/2-1), 1h 29m 28.532s, 124.406 mph
Retired, A. Prost (MP4/2-2), gearbox pinion bearing

German Grand Prix, Hockenheim,
5 August, 185.83 miles
1st, A. Prost (MP4/2-3), 1h 24m 43.210s, 131.608 mph
2nd, N. Lauda (MP4/2-1)

Austrian Grand Prix, Österreichring,
19 August, 188.313 miles
1st, N. Lauda (MP4/2-1), 1h 21m 12.851s, 139.11 mph
Retired, A. Prost (MP4/2-2), spin

Dutch Grand Prix, Zandvoort,
26 August, 187.586 miles
1st, A. Prost (MP4/2-2), 1h 37m 21.468s, 115.606 mph
2nd, N. Lauda (MP4/2-1)

Italian Grand Prix, Monza, 9 September,
183.801 miles
1st, N. Lauda (MP4/2-1), 1h 20m 29.065s, 137.021 mph
Retired, A. Prost (MP4/2-3), turbocharger

European Grand Prix, Nürburgring,
7 October, 189.091 miles
1st, A. Prost (MP4/2-2), 1h 35m 13.284s, 119.148 mph
4th, N. Lauda (MP4/2-1)

Portuguese Grand Prix, Estoril,
21 October, 189.207 miles
1st, A. Prost (MP4/2-2), 1h 41m 11.753s, 112.182 mph
2nd, N. Lauda (MP4/2-1)

Drivers' World Championship:
1st, N. Lauda, 72 points
2nd, A. Prost, 71.5 points

Constructors' Cup:
1st, McLaren, 143.5 points

1985

Brazilian Grand Prix, Rio de Janeiro,
7 April, 190.692 miles
1st, A. Prost (MP4/2B-5), 1h 41m 26.115s, 112.795 mph
Retired, N. Lauda (MP4/2B-4), fuel metering unit

Portuguese Grand Prix, Estoril, 21 April,
181.098 miles (race stopped short)
Retired, A. Prost (MP4/2B-5), spin
Retired, N. Lauda (MP4/2B-4), piston failure

San Marino Grand Prix, Imola, 5 May,
187.90 miles
4th, N. Lauda (MP4/2B-4), 1 lap in arrears
Disqualified, A. Prost (MP4/2B-5), car underweight

Monaco Grand Prix, Monte Carlo,
19 May, 160.522 miles
1st, A. Prost (MP4/2B-5), 1h 51m 58.034s, 86.018 mph
Retired, N. Lauda (MP4/2B-4), spin

Canadian Grand Prix, Circuit Gilles Villeneuve, Montreal, 16 June,
191.82 miles
3rd, A. Prost (MP4/2B-5)
Retired, N. Lauda (MP4/2B-4), engine overheating

United States Grand Prix (Detroit),
Detroit, 23 June, 157.500 miles
Retired, N. Lauda (MP4/2B-4), brakes
Retired, A. Prost (MP4/2B-5), brakes/accident

French Grand Prix, Paul Ricard, 7 July,
191.337 miles
3rd, A. Prost (MP4/2B-5)
Retired, N. Lauda (MP4/2B-4), gearbox

British Grand Prix, Silverstone, 21 July,
190.580 miles (race stopped short)
1st, A. Prost (MP4/2B-2), 1h 18m 10.436s, (146.274 mph)
Retired, N. Lauda (MP4/2B-4), electrics

German Grand Prix, Nürburgring,
4 August, 189.091 miles
2nd, A. Prost (MP4/2B-2)
5th, N. Lauda (MP4/2B-4)

Austrian Grand Prix, Österreichring,
18 August, 191.993 miles
1st, A. Prost (MP4/2B-3), 1h 20m 12.583s, 143.618 mph
Retired, N. Lauda (MP4/2B-4), turbocharger

Dutch Grand Prix, Zandvoort,
25 August, 184.944 miles
1st, N. Lauda (MP4/2B-4), 1h 32m 29.263s, 119.979 mph
2nd, A. Prost (MP4/2B-3)

Italian Grand Prix, Monza, 8 September, 183.801 miles
1st, A. Prost (MP42/2B-5), 1h 17m 59.451s, 141.402 mph
Retired, N. Lauda (MP4/2B-4), engine

Belgian Grand Prix, Spa-Francorchamps, 15 September, 185.669 miles
3rd, A. Prost (MP4/2B-5)
Did not start, N. Lauda (MP4/2B-4), wrist injury in practice

European Grand Prix, Brands Hatch, 6 October, 196.050 miles
4th, A. Prost (MP4/2B-2)
7th, J. Watson (MP4/2B-4), 2 laps in arrears

South African Grand Prix, Kyalami, 19 October, 191.247 miles
3rd, A. Prost (MP4/2B-6)
Retired, N. Lauda (MP4/2B-4), turbocharger

Australian Grand Prix, Adelaide, 3 November, 192.498 miles
Retired, A. Prost (MP4/2B-6), turbocharger
Retired, N. Lauda (MP4/2B-4), accident

Drivers' World Championship:
1st, A. Prost, 73 points (76 gross)
10th, N. Lauda, 14 points

Constructors' Cup:
1st, McLaren, 90 points

1986

Brazilian Grand Prix, Rio de Janeiro, 23 March, 190.692 miles
Retired, K. Rosberg (MP4/2C-2), piston failure
Retired, A. Prost (MP4/2C-3), piston failure

Spanish Grand Prix, Jerez, 13 April, 188.708 miles
3rd, A. Prost (MP4/2C-3)
4th, K. Rosberg (MP4/2C-2), 1 lap in arrears

San Marino Grand Prix, Imola, 27 April, 187.90 miles
1st, A. Prost (MP4/2C-3), 1h 32m 28.408s, 121.918 mph
5th, K. Rosberg (MP4/2C-2), 2 laps in arrears, not running at the finish, ran out of fuel

Monaco Grand Prix, Monte Carlo, 11 May, 161.298 miles
1st, A. Prost (MP4/2C-3), , 1h 55m 41.060s, 83.657 mph
2nd, K. Rosberg (MP4/2C-2)

Belgian Grand Prix, Spa-Francorchamps, 25 May, 185.429 miles
6th, A. Prost (MP4/2C-3)
Retired, K. Rosberg (MP4/2C-2), engine

Canadian Grand Prix, Circuit Gilles Villeneuve, Montreal, 15 June, 189.07 miles
2nd, A. Prost (MP4/2C-3)
4th, K. Rosberg (MP4/2C-2)

United States Grand Prix (Detroit), Detroit, 22 June, 157.500 miles
3rd, A. Prost (MP4/2C-3)
Retired, K. Rosberg (MP4/2C-2), transmission

French Grand Prix, Paul Ricard, 6 July, 189.543 miles
2nd, A. Prost (MP4/2C-3)
4th, K. Rosberg (MP4/2C-2)

British Grand Prix, Brands Hatch, 13 July, 196.050 miles
3rd, A. Prost (MP4/2C-3), 1 lap in arrears
Retired, K. Rosberg (MP4/2C-2), gearbox

German Grand Prix, Hockenheim, 27 July, 185.83 miles
5th, K. Rosberg (MP4/2C-2), 1 lap in arrears, not running at the finish, out of fuel
6th, A. Prost (MP4/2C-3), 1 lap in arrears, not running at the finish, out of fuel

Hungarian Grand Prix, Hungaroring, 10 August, 189.557 miles
Retired, A. Prost (MP4/2C-4), accident
Retired, K. Rosberg (MP4/2C-2), rear suspension

Austrian Grand Prix, Österreichring, 17 August, 191.933 miles
1st, A. Prost (MP4/2C-3), 1h 21m 22.531s, 141.561 mph
9th, K. Rosberg (MP4/2C-2), 5 laps in arrears, not running at the finish, electrics

Italian Grand Prix, Monza, 7 September, 183.801 miles
4th, A. Rosberg (MP4/2C-2)
Disqualified, A. Prost (MP4/2C-3)

Portuguese Grand Prix, Estoril, 21 September, 189.207 miles
2nd, A. Prost (MP4/2C-1)
Retired, K. Rosberg (MP4/2C-2), engine

Mexican Grand Prix, Hermanos Rodriguez, 12 October, 186.801 miles
2nd, A. Prost (MP4/2C-5)
Retired, K. Rosberg (MP4/2C-2), puncture

Australian Grand Prix, Adelaide, 26 October, 192.498 miles
1st, A. Prost (MP4/2C-5), 1h 54m 20.388s, 101.040 mph
Retired, K. Rosberg (MP4/2C-2), tyre failure

Drivers' World Championship:
1st, A. Prost, 72 points (74 gross)
6th, K. Rosberg, 22 points

Constructors' Cup:
2nd, McLaren, 96 points

1987

Brazilian Grand Prix, Rio de Janeiro, 12 April, 190.692 miles
1st, A. Prost (MP4/3-3), 1h 39m 45.141s, 114.699 mph
3rd, S. Johansson (MP4/3-2)

San Marino Grand Prix, Imola, 3 May, 185.30 miles
4th, S. Johansson (MP4/3-2)
Retired, A. Prost (MP4/3-3), alternator

Belgian Grand Prix, Spa-Francorchamps, 17 May, 185.429 miles
1st, A. Prost (MP4/3-3), 1h 27m 03.217s, 127.803 mph
2nd, S. Johansson (MP4/3-2)

Monaco Grand Prix, Monte Carlo, 31 May, 161.298 miles
9th, A. Prost (MP4/3-3), 3 laps in arrears, not running at the finish, engine
Retired, S. Johansson (MP4/3-2), engine

United States Grand Prix (Detroit), Detroit, 21 June, 157.500 miles
3rd, A. Prost (MP4/3-3)
7th, S. Johansson (MP4/3-2), 3 laps in arrears

French Grand Prix, Paul Ricard, 5 July, 189.543 miles
3rd, A. Prost (MP4/3-3)
8th, S. Johansson (MP4/3-2), 6 laps in arrears, not running at the finish, alternator belt

British Grand Prix, Silverstone, 12 July, 192.985 miles
Retired, A. Prost (MP4/3-4), broken clutch bearing/electrics
Retired, S. Johansson (MP4/3-2), turbocharger

German Grand Prix, Hockenheim, 26 July, 185.83 miles
2nd, S. Johansson (MP4/3-2)
7th, A. Prost (MP4/3-4), 5 laps in arrears, not running at the finish, alternator belt

Hungarian Grand Prix, Hungaroring, 9 August, 189.557 miles
3rd, A. Prost (MP4/3-4)
Retired, S. Johansson (MP4/3-2), seized differential

Austrian Grand Prix, Österreichring, 16 August, 191.993 miles
6th, A. Prost (MP4/3-4), 2 laps in arrears
7th, S. Johansson (MP4/3-3), 2 laps in arrears

Italian Grand Prix, Monza, 6 September, 180.197 miles
6th, S. Johnasson (MP4/3-5)
15th, A. Prost (MP4/3-4), 4 laps in arrears

Portuguese Grand Prix, Estoril, 21 September, 189.207 miles
1st, A. Prost (MP4/3-4), 1h 37m 03.906s, 116.957 mph
5th, S. Johansson (MP4/3-5), 1 lap in arrears

Spanish Grand Prix, Jerez, 27 September, 188.708 miles
2nd, A. Prost (MP4/3-4)
3rd, S. Johansson (MP4/3-5)

Mexican Grand Prix, Hermanos Rodriguez, 18 October, 173.065 miles
Retired, S. Johansson (MP4/3-3), accident
Retired, A. Prost (MP4/3-4), accident

Japanese Grand Prix, Suzuka, 1 November, 185.670 miles
3rd, S. Johansson (MP4/3-5)
7th, A. Prost (MP4/3-4), 1 lap in arrears

Australian Grand Prix, Adelaide, 15 November, 192.454 miles
Retired, S. Johansson (MP4/3-5), brakes
Retired, A. Prost (MP4/3-4), brakes

Drivers' World Championship:
4th, A. Prost, 46 points
6th, S. Johansson, 30 points

Constructors' Cup:
2nd, McLaren, 76 points

1988

Brazilian Grand Prix, Rio de Janeiro, 3 April, 187.566 miles
1st, A. Prost (MP4/4-2), 1h 36m 06.857s, 117.089 mph
Disqualified, A. Senna (MP4/4-3), changing cars after green flag shown

San Marino Grand Prix, Imola, 1 May, 187.902 miles
1st, A. Senna (MP4/4-1), 1h 32m 41.264s, 121.635 mph
2nd, A. Prost (MP4/4-4)

Monaco Grand Prix, Monte Carlo, 15 May, 161.298 miles
1st, A. Prost (MP4/4-4), 1h 57m 17.077s, 82.516 mph
Retired, A. Senna (MP4/4-1), accident

Mexican Grand Prix, Mexico City, 29 May, 184.054 miles
1st, A. Prost (MP4/4-4), 1h 30m 15.737s, 122.346 mph
2nd, A. Senna (MP4/4-1)

Canadian Grand Prix, Circuit Gilles Villeneuve, Montreal, 12 June, 188.21 miles
1st, A. Senna (MP4/4-1), 1h 39m 46.618s, 113.183 mph
2nd, A. Prost (MP4/4)

United States Grand Prix (Detroit), Detroit, 19 June, 157.500 miles
1st, A. Senna (MP4/4-2), 1h 54m 56.035s, 82.221 mph
2nd, A. Prost (MP4/4-4)

French Grand Prix, Paul Ricard, 3 July, 189.543 miles
1st, A. Prost (MP4/4-4), 1h 37m 37.328s, 116.495 mph
2nd, A. Senna (MP4/4-2)

British Grand Prix, Silverstone, 10 July, 192.985 miles
1st, A. Senna (MP4/4-5), 1h 33m 16.367s, 124.142 mph
Retired, A. Prost (MP4/4-4), handling problems

German Grand Prix, Hockenheim, 24 July, 185.83 miles
1st, A. Senna (MP4/4-5), 1h 32m 54.188s, 120.016 mph
2nd, A. Prost (MP4/4-4)

Hungarian Grand Prix, Hungaroring, 7 August, 189.557 miles
1st, A. Senna (MP4/4-5), 1h 57m 47.081s, 96.561 mph
2nd, A. Prost (MP4/4-4)

Belgian Grand Prix, Spa-Francorchamps, 28 August, 185.429 miles
1st, A. Senna (MP4/4-5), 1h 28m 00.549s, 126.415 mph
2nd, A. Prost (MP4/4-4)

Italian Grand Prix, Monza, 11 September, 183.801 miles
10th, A. Senna (MP4/4-5), 2 laps in arrears, not running at the finish, spin
Retired, A. Prost (MP4/4-4), engine

Portuguese Grand Prix, Estoril, 25 September, 189.207 miles
1st, A. Prost (MP4/4-6), 1h 37m 40.958s, 116.217 mph
6th, A. Senna (MP4/4-5)

Spanish Grand Prix, Jerez, 2 October, 188.708 miles
1st, A. Prost (MP4/4-6), 1h 48m 43.851s, 104.133 mph
4th, A. Senna (MP4/4-5)

Japanese Grand Prix, Suzuka, 30 October, 185.670 miles
1st, A. Senna (MP4/4-2), 1hr 33m 26.173s, 119.230 mph
2nd, A. Prost (MP4/4-6)

Australian Grand Prix, Adelaide, 13 November, 192.498 miles
1st, A. Prost (MP4/4-6), 1h 53m 14.676s, 102.044 mph
2nd, A. Senna (MP4/4-2)

Drivers' World Championship:
1st, A. Senna, 90 points (94 gross)
2nd, A. Prost, 87 points (105 gross)

Constructors' Cup:
1st, McLaren, 199 points

1989

Brazilian Grand Prix, Autodromo Nelson Piquet, Rio de Janeiro, 26 March, 190.692 miles
2nd, A. Prost (MP4/5-3)
11th, A. Senna (MP4/5-2), 2 laps in arrears

San Marino Grand Prix, Imola, 23 April, 191.033 miles
1st, A. Senna (MP4/5-1), 1h 26m 51.245s, 125.479 mph
2nd, A. Prost (MP4/5-3)

Monaco Grand Prix, Monte Carlo, 7 May, 159.236 miles
1st, A. Senna (MP4/5-1), 1h 53m 33.251s, 84.134 mph
2nd, A. Prost (MP4/5-3)

Mexican Grand Prix, Hermanos Rodriguez, 28 May, 189.548 miles
1st, A. Senna (MP4/5-1), 1h 35m 21.43s, 119.194 mph
5th, A. Prost (MP4/5-3)

United States Grand Prix, Phoenix, 4 June, 177.000 miles
1st, A. Prost (MP4/5-3), 2h 01m 33.133s, 87.370 mph
Retired, A. Senna (MP4/5-4), engine misfire

Canadian Grand Prix, Circuit Gilles Villeneuve, Montreal, 18 June, 188.23 miles
7th, A. Senna (MP4/5-4), 3 laps in arrears, not running at the finish, engine failure
Retired, A. Prost (MP4/5-3), chassis damage

French Grand Prix, Paul Ricard, 9 July, 189.543 miles
1st, A. Prost (MP4/5-5), 1h 38m 29.411s, 115.469 mph
Retired, A. Senna (MP4/5-4), differential

British Grand Prix, Silverstone, 16 July, 190.080 miles
1st, A. Prost (MP4/5-5), 1h 19m 22.131s, 143.694 mph
Retired, A. Senna (MP4/5-6), spun off

German Grand Prix, Hockenheim, 30 July, 190.055 miles
1st, A. Senna (MP4/5-3), 1h 21m 43.302s, 139.455 mph
2nd, A. Prost (MP4/5-5)

Hungarian Grand Prix, Hungaroring, 13 August, 189.850 miles
2nd, A. Senna (MP4/5-3)
4th, A. Prost (MP4/5-5)

Belgian Grand Prix, Spa-Francorchamps, 27 August, 189.741 miles
1st, A. Senna (MP4/5-7), 1h 40m 54.196s, 112.758 mph
2nd, A. Prost (MP4/5-5)

Italian Grand Prix, Monza, 10 September, 191.012 miles
1st, A. Prost (MP4/5-5), 1h 19m 27.550s, 144.145 mph
Retired, A. Senna (MP4/5-7), engine

Portuguese Grand Prix, Estoril, 24 September, 191.91 miles
2nd, A. Prost (MP4/5-5)
Retired, A. Senna (MP4/5-7), collision with Mansell

Spanish Grand Prix, Jerez, 1 October, 191.333 miles
1st, A. Senna (MP4/5-7), 1h 47m 48.264s, 106.543 mph
3rd, A. Prost (MP4/5-5)

Japanese Grand Prix, Suzuka, 22 October, 192.973 miles
Retired, A. Prost (MP4/5-8), collision with Senna
Disqualified, A. Senna (MP4/5-7), after collision with Prost

Australian Grand Prix, Adelaide, 5 November, 190.27 miles
Retired, A. Senna (MP4/5-7), accident with Brundle
Retired, A. Prost (MP4/5-8), driver withdrew

Drivers' World Championship:
1st, A. Prost, 76 points (81 gross)
2nd, A. Senna, 60 points

Constructors' Cup:
1st, McLaren, 141 points

Appendix 2

Specifications of McLaren Cars, 1983-90

Model	**MP4/1E**	**MP4/2**	**MP4/2B**	**MP4/2C**	**MP4/3**
Year raced	1983	1984	1985	1986	1987
Number Built	3 (plus MP4/1D test hack)	4	6	5	6
Engine make	TAG PO1	TAG PO1	TAG PO1	TAG PO1	TAG PO1
Layout	V6	V6	V6	V6	V6
Capacity (bore and stroke)	1499 cc (82 x 47 mm)	1499 cc (82 x 47 mm)	1499 cc (82 x 47 mm)	1499 cc (82 x 47 mm)	1499 cc (82 x 47 mm)
Turbocharger	KKK (2)	KKK (2)	KKK (2)	KKK (2)	KKK (2)
Fuel injection	Bosch Motronic	Bosch Motronic	Bosch Motronic	Bosch Motronic	Bosch Motronic
Ignition	Bosch Motronic	Bosch Motronic	Bosch Motronic	Bosch Motronic	Bosch Motronic
Bhp at rpm	700 bhp at 11,500 rpm	750 bhp at 11,500 rpm	750 bhp at 12,000 rpm	800 bhp at 12,000 rpm	850 bhp at 12,000 rpm
Transmission	5-speed	5-speed	5-speed	5-speed	6-speed
Front Suspension	Push-rods, inboard auxiliary rockers, lower wishbones, inboard springs	Push-rods, inboard auxiliary rockers lower wishbones, inboard springs	Push-rods, inboard auxiliary rockers, upper and lower wishbones, inboard springs	Push-rods, inboard auxiliary rockers, upper and lower wishbones, inboard springs	Push-rods, inboard auxiliary rockers, upper and lower wishbones, inboard springs
Rear Suspension	Upper rocker arms, lower wishbones, inboard springs	Upper rocker arms, lower wishbones, inboard springs	Push-rods, inboards auxiliary rockers, upper and lower wishbones, inboard springs	Push-rods, inboard auxiliary rockers, upper and lower wishbones, inboard springs	Push-rods, inboard auxiliary rockers, upper and lower wishbones, inboard springs
Wheelbase	105.8 in (2687 mm)	110 in (2794 mm)	110 in (2794 mm)	110 in (2794 mm)	110 in (2794 mm)
Front track	71.5 in (1816 mm)	71.5 in (1816 mm)	71.5 in (1816 mm)	71.5 in (1816 mm)	71.5 in (1816 mm)
Rear track	66.0 in (1676 mm)	66.0 in (1676 mm)	66.0 in (1676 mm)	66.0 in (1676 mm)	66.0 in (1676 mm)

Model	MP4/4	MP4/5
Year raced	1988	1989
Number Built	6	8
Engine make	Honda RA168-E	Honda RA109E
Layout	V6	V10
Capacity (bore and stroke)	1499 cc (79 x 50.8 mm)	3490 cc (92 x 52.5 mm)
Turbocharger	IHI (2)	–
Fuel Injection	Honda PGM F1	Honda PGM 1G
Ignition	Honda PGM F1	Honda PGM 1G
Bhp at rpm	900 bhp at 12,500 rpm	685 bhp
Transmission	6-speed	6-speed
Front Suspension	Pull-rods, double wishbones, inboard springs	Pull-rods, double wishbones, inboard springs
Rear Suspension	Push-rods, double wishbones, inboard springs	Push-rods, double wishbones, inboard springs
Wheelbase	113 in (2870 mm)	114 in (2896 mm)
Front track	71.0 in (1803 mm)	71.6 in (1820 mm)
Rear track	66.0 in (1676 mm)	67.5 in (1670 mm)